The Prospect of Heaven

Musings of an enquiring believer

Frederick Levison

First Published 1997

ISBN 0 947988 73 4

We gratefully acknowledge the contribution of
THE DRUMMOND TRUST
3 PITT TERRACE, STIRLING
towards the publication costs of this book

Published by Wild Goose Publications

Wild Goose Publications, Unit 15, Six Harmony Row, Glasgow G51 3BA
Wild Goose Publications is the publishing division of the Iona Community.
Scottish Charity No. SC003794. Limited Company Reg. No SCO96243.
Distributed in Australia and New Zealand by Willow Connection Pty Ltd,
Unit 7A, 3-9 Kenneth Road, Manly Vale NSW 2093.
Permission to reproduce any part of this work in Australia or New Zealand
should be sought from Willow Connection.
A catalogue record for this book is available from the British Library.
Printed by The Cromwell Press Ltd, Melksham, Wilts.

*For my loved ones in heaven
who are still with me in the communion of saints*

The cover image — the North Arch of the Saint Kentigern Tapestry — is by the late Robert Stewart of Loch Striven, Argyll. Robert Stewart was Head of the Design School and Deputy Director of Glasgow School of Art. The image is one panel of a triptych which hangs in Glasgow Cathedral.

Robert Stewart described the tapestry in this way: 'In the tapestry, very ancient symbols are linked with and unified by the central representation of the Church: all the elements are inter-related, and the position of each symbol contributes to the meaning of the whole ... In the North arch are the Sun, supporter of life, and fire, and the burning bush. Over and above the detailed symbolism they contain, the North and South arches are intended to glorify the creation of the universe and to praise the immensity of that creation.'

The tapestry was woven at the Dovecot Studios in Corstorphine by the Edinburgh Tapestry Company Ltd and completed in August 1979.

Wild Goose Publications would like to thank Sheila Stewart, Malcolm McCoig, the Friends of Glasgow Cathedral and the Dovecot Studios for their kindness in supporting this title.

'Well, modern theologians tend to be a bit shifty about the afterlife, I'm afraid. Even Catholic ones.'

'Really?'

'Take Küng's *On Being a Christian*, for example, one of the modern classics. You won't find anything in the index under "Afterlife" or "Heaven".'

'I don't see the point of religion if there's no heaven', said Ursula. ... 'And what about hell? Has that gone down the tubes too?'

'Very largely, and good riddance, I'd say.'

'And purgatory with it, I guess?'

'Oddly enough, modern theologians, even non-Catholic ones, are rather more sympathetic towards the idea of purgatory, though there's very little scriptural warrant for it.'

(David Lodge, *Paradise News*, p. 205)

Contents

1

To fill the void

*'If we are to live in any deep sense fruitfully and
strongly, our horizons must include the life to come
and our souls feel the impact of those realms beyond
space and time towards which we move.'*

attributed to Revd Dr A.C. Craig[1]

One of my daughters is a Doubting Thomas, and shares
the scepticism of so many people today about an afterlife.
'You'll have to convince me,' she says. Hence this book.

I am also motivated by the desire to clarify my own mind on matters
seldom explored by contemporary theologians; and to say to the
Church at large, Look, do you know you have a hang-up about heaven
and that there is a seeping scepticism among your own members?

To persuade unbelievers is a formidable task. Jesus himself said of
the sceptics of his day, 'They would not be convinced though one rose
from the dead'. And it is no good beginning with the Resurrection,
however central that is to Christianity, because people today are not
prepared to believe six impossible things before breakfast, or even one.

Cumulative evidence is a better starting-point, although paranormal experience doesn't take us far. But when you throw in the sacramental nature of the universe (although this requires the eye of faith),
the purposeful nature of history and our individual strivings, the
mystery and marvel of human beings, both saints and sinners, and all
the hints and guesses you can glean from poets, musicians, artists, mystics
and the wisdom and revelations of Scripture, there is a substantial body
of reputable belief as opposed to mere credulity.

In the end, however, I have to agree with the theologian John Burnaby when he says, 'We believe in the life to come, not because man is what he is, but because God is what He is.'[2] The key to belief in the afterlife is faith, not a vague hope but faith in a God who cares for us so much that he cannot possibly let us perish.

With heedless inconsistency many say, Oh yes, we believe in God, in some kind of invisible spiritual Being, but not in a life beyond this one. They don't see that the two go hand in hand. What kind of useless god do they believe in if he demolishes us at death? Surely not 'the Lord God Almighty, Maker of heaven and earth'. And if there is no God, or it is a matter of indifference to you and he is, literally, neither here nor there, then heaven can only be what the ill-fated lovers sing about in *West Side Story*, a compensatory myth, a land of heart's desire, somewhere beyond the demands and sorrows of this tortured world.

Heaven has no validity apart from the validity of God, and clear-minded doubters see this. Thus we find Seamus Heaney, the distinguished poet and Oxford professor, saying in an interview: 'My language and my sensibility is yearning to admit a kind of religious or transcendental dimension. But then there's the reality: there's no heaven, no afterlife of the sort we were promised and no personal god.'[3]

A character in one of Julian Barnes's novels asks, 'Hey you up there in the sky, is anyone home?'[4] Is anyone home, not in the sky (forget that) but in heaven? That is the crux question.

A book about heaven must therefore be a book about God, whose existence and nature no mere hunch can establish. We need the testimony of religions and of those whose faith conveys a reality and authority more convincing than our own. Most of all, it is through Christ, whose whole life and teaching reveal 'the human face of God', that the Heavenly Father becomes accessible and guarantees the afterlife.

There are books on heaven which explore the world's religions and philosophies and the beliefs of many ethnic groups. This is beyond my scope and must be left to more exact scholars in fuller volumes. I shall, however, quote many humble saints, though not the fundamentalists of any religion. And I shall keep almost entirely to the Christian tradition, its definitive expression in the Old and New Testaments and later reflections within the Church.

Some of my friends seem to be alarmed that, having dealt with the existence of heaven I might be tempted to describe it. To speculate about the nature of the life to come is, they say, presumptuous and sacrilegious. Do not the scriptures draw a veil? And, in any case, a life beyond time and space is beyond our perceptions. We should be content to remain silent.

A careful reading of the Bible, however, shows that there are chinks in the veil. I do not think it is irreverent to probe these, together with the 'hints and guesses' of the eternal in our earthly existence, provided we do not carry speculation too far, and also admit that any human predictions may prove wide of the mark, if not entirely wrong.

Heaven is a topic that sets alarm bells ringing, because thinking seriously about it can lead to spiritualism, or to ancient errors like the invocation of saints and prayers for the dead.

But contrary alarm bells are also ringing and no-one takes much notice. These bells tell us that the Church has hurt itself and deprived its members by neglecting heaven. The sense of the numinous, of that awe-inspiring mystery of which Rudolf Otto wrote in *The Idea of the Holy,* is absent from much of our worship. On Trinity Sunday, for example, a high day in the Christian calendar when the Church could be ablaze with the glory of God and worshippers see the Lord as Isaiah saw him 'high and lifted up' in majesty (*Isaiah 6:1*), many preachers try to 'unscrew the inscrutable' and explain the mystery of the Trinity with threefold analogies. They only succeed in trivializing what is holy, and perhaps it is this, rather than boredom, that turns away the young. And when our God is too small and we turn to trivialities and lose touch with the holy we also distance ourselves from heaven.

Even the Roman Catholic Church, which for centuries was vividly aware of saints and angels, paradise and purgatory, has not entirely survived the onset of secularism. At a gathering of clergy in Scotland, a speaker said,

> 'We're dealing with a completely asphyxiating culture. The symbol of the change is the biting off by the devil, through the media, of the final words of the Creed, "and the life of the world to come". The common assumption of so many of us, and of fifty per cent of our congregations, is that when you're dead you're dead.'[5]

What has happened, I believe, is that once it was realized that the threat of hellfire was both invalid and incompatible with the grace of the gospel, hell was abandoned and heaven, by inference, discredited and quietly demoted from its prominence on the Church's agenda.

The result is a void in our worship. Commemoration of the blessed dead and rejoicing in the communion of saints are missing from most of our services. We raise our hearts and minds to God but not very often to the Church Triumphant of those in heaven.

Yet in a post-Christian culture where many have abandoned belief in God there is still a spiritual searching, shown in an interest in the psychic and paranormal and a wide variety of beliefs and cults. A society that regards itself as rational and enlightened and rejects miracles, says Melanie Phillips, 'is veering into superstitions and gobbledygook'.[6] I believe the answer to this misdirected spirituality is a Church which proclaims loud and clear the Christian hope of the life everlasting.

I am optimistic that this hope will revive in the next generations, including my daughter's. For there is, even in this secular and sceptical age, a spiritual hunger and a search for meaning, even if our answers have not yet found acceptance. This is a challenge to contemporary theologians who have paid too little attention to the transcendental and eschatology (i.e. the doctrine of the last things, the final destiny of the individual and of humankind). It is a challenge also to the Churches to revive that sense of wonder and awareness of the unseen that is one of our basic needs.

How can we give a lead without a larger vision? Recent efforts by the Churches to revitalize worship, restate the faith and resuscitate evangelism, admirable though these are, do not go far enough. Their revival will be incomplete, even abortive, unless they reintroduce an eager anticipation of heaven, to remind us that we are its citizens and enable us to participate even now in the communion of saints.

1. Attributed to Revd Dr A. C. Craig
2. John Burnaby, *The Belief of Christendom: A Commentary on the Nicene Creed* (London: SPCK, 1959) p. 192
3. The *Financial Times* (1 June 1991)
4. Julian Barnes, *A History of the World in 10½ Chapters* (Basingstoke: Pan Paperback, 1990) p. 212
5. Reported in the journal *Open House* (December 1991)
6. Melanie Phillips, The *Observer* (3 July 1994)

2

Hints and guesses

*'For most of us there is only the unattended
Moment, the moment in and out of time,
The distraction fit, lost in a shaft of sunlight,
The wild thyme unseen, or the winter lightning
Or the waterfall, or music heard so deeply
That it is not heard at all, but you are the music
While the music lasts. These are only hints and
guesses, Hints followed by guesses...'*

T. S. Eliot[1]

There are no proofs of the afterlife but there are hints and guesses; hints which may make us question and guess at what lies beyond our mortal sight.

Heaven is not quite 'The undiscovered country from whose bourn/ No traveller returns'.[2] Some — and not only Lazarus, whose backward look was caught in a statue by the sculptor Jacob Epstein — have returned from near-death experiences. Those who have report light at the end of the tunnel, but they have glimpsed only the threshold: none of them have penetrated the inner rooms, and they have nothing to describe.

You do not need to die to see that light for it is evident in our present existence. Every artist knows this, although most are reluctant to ascribe it to God. People who deny any realm of spirit beyond the material world repudiate the testimony not only of religious believers but of the innumerable writers, artists and musicians down the ages who have affirmed it. These have ranged from Socrates asserting the after-death existence of the soul to the visions of Dante, Milton and Blake; from Robert Vaughan, who 'felt through all this fleshly dress/ Bright shoots of everlastingnesse'[3], and the other metaphysical poets of the seventeenth century, to Wordsworth and Francis Thompson's 'In No Strange Land'; from Chesterton and Eliot, Auden and Edwin Muir to Kathleen Raine and Charles Causley.

Include the clergy, and the testimony is even more impressive. An agnostic may discount them as having a vested interest in the unseen. To myself, however, Augustine talking to his mother, Donne and Herbert, Newman (in *Gerontius* as well as in 'Lead Kindly Light'), Claudel, Gerard Manley Hopkins, R. S. Thomas and George MacLeod (in the poetry of his prayers), corroborate that there are moments which give us what Eliot has called 'a tremor of bliss, a wink of heaven, a whisper'.[4]

Certain places like Iona, that 'thin place' hallowed by St Columba, and other haunts of pilgrimage such as Assisi and Galilee, Lindisfarne and Lourdes, have an aura of spirituality, a transparency; so do many churches hallowed by prayer and the faith of their builders.

At Chartres or York Minster the glowing glass and soaring space create a feeling of eternity; and though their many monuments may only suggest a sombre mausoleum to the unbeliever, for those with faith they give faces to the communion of saints. These, like the pilgrim sites, are of course exceptional places, but ordinary churches too can bring heaven near. Those with thrusting spires and gothic arches are especially evocative, whereas many contemporary buildings, squat, low-ceilinged and built of brick do little to suggest the transcendent. But because Jesus meets with his followers there and because the Word is proclaimed and prayer said, these are more than meeting-rooms; they are sanctuaries, houses of God and therefore windows to heaven.

Music and the visual arts are equally luminous. We need only think of the musicians Bach and Handel, the painters Giotto and Rembrandt, and craftsmen in glass and metal, wood and stone.

It is not that creative works have to be religiously motivated in order to signify the eternal; it is enough that they are inspired. Although the painter van Gogh, for instance, lost the Christian faith he had once passionately held, his religious feeling remained. He wrote, 'I want to paint men and women with that something of the eternal which the halo used to symbolize, and which we now seek to give by the actual radiance and vibrancy of our colouring.'[5]

The witness of the natural world is even more impressive. No human-made artistry or design can surpass the designs of nature from which all human forms derive. No scientific explanation of a snowflake, a butterfly's wing, a leaf or a flower can account for their beauty. 'Even Solomon in all his glory was not clothed like one of these' (*Matthew 6:29*). And though a painter like Constable or Corot can marvellously emulate a tree, they cannot create one. To the philosopher, beauty may be only in the eye of the beholder, but to the poet Keats it was truth, and for many people a phrase from the Jewish writer and mystic Simone Weil defines it luminously: 'Beauty is eternity here below.'[6] In R. S. Thomas' felicitous phrase: 'Eternity wearing the green leaves of time.'[7]

At the close of John McGrath's television play *The Long Roads*, an elderly Highlander, whose wife lies dying, stands outside their cottage in Skye, gazing across the rough pasture of the wide machair and the shining sea to the distant hills and holding back his tears. He cries, 'Oh God, why did You make the world so beautiful — and then make us leave it?'[8] Only a puritan would reply that such beauty is transient, merely an earthly treasure which we should count as loss. If we have had our eyes opened to the glory of nature by St Francis or St Columba, the psalmists before them, ancient Chinese art, the aesthetic awakening of the nineteenth and twentieth centuries, or any other means, the Highlander's question is a real one, which shares John Baillie's perception that 'Nature is not an argument for God but is a sacrament of Him'[9]. At death we shall not discard the world's beauty, for it is a hint or intimation of heaven where, I believe, it will be both conserved and surpassed.

'The world's beauty' is a misleading phrase. For, as C. S. Lewis points out in his sermon 'The Weight of Glory', the things

> 'in which we thought the beauty was located will betray us if we trust to them; it was not *in* them, it only came *through* them ... For they are not the thing itself; they are only the scent of a flower we have not found, the echo of a tune we have not heard, news from a country we have never yet visited. ... We are summoned to pass in through Nature, beyond her, into that splendour which she fitfully reflects'.[10]

It takes faith to see this; and faith, it has been said, is interpretation. If the sceptics only had the willingness and the imagination to interpret what stares them in the face they would discover heaven.

Compared to the test-tube the imagination might seem an arbitrary measure of truth, but the playwright George Bernard Shaw was probably right when he made St Joan answer those who derided her visions by saying that her 'voices' came from God. 'They come from your imagination', they told her. 'Of course', she replied. 'That is how the messages of God come to us.' Later in Shaw's play, the Dauphin asks her, 'Why don't the voices come to me?' 'They do come to you', she says, 'but you do not hear them. You have not sat in the field in the evening listening for them. When the angelus rings you cross yourself and have done with it; but if you prayed from your heart, and listened to the thrilling of the bells in the air after they stop ringing, you would hear the voices as well as I do.'[11]

'Earth's crammed with heaven' in the words of Elizabeth Barrett Browning. It seems that we fail to see the signs, perhaps because we do not take time to stand and stare. Or it may be through our very zest for living. We strive too hard after reality, living a full social, mental and physical life but without direction; leaving little room for God's lightning to strike. 'Where we permit ourselves to become hopelessly limited by our narrow vision', said Donnie Munro, the Rector of Edinburgh University, in his valedictory address in February 1994, 'we fall into the trap of the collector of rare butterflies, who one day sees one of the rarest known breeds and sets about capturing his prize. For many hours without success he pursues the object of his desire until at last, tired and defeated in his task, he sits down to rest, at which point the elusive butterfly lands on his head. In the unguarded moment, when least expected, we are afforded glimpses of the power and the mystery of faith.'[12]

Hints of heaven in the arts and in nature can be demonstrated by an abundance of quotations. A more immediate witness is that of self-knowledge and the observation of others. Our capacity to give and receive love has led many to reflect, like Eliot, that 'Friendship should be more than biting Time can sever'.[13] And when, at its deepest level, friendship is the falling in love of two persons and their enduring devotion, to describe that relationship only in terms of mental, psychological and physical affinity is, to say the least, implausible. It will contain these elements, yes, but its essence is spiritual. As Iris Murdoch wrote,

> 'The foreverness of real love is one of the reasons why even unrequited love is a source of joy. The human soul craves for the eternal of which, apart from certain rare mysteries of religion, only love and art can give a glimpse.'[14]

Young people in love use metaphors to describe what has happened to them. It is 'walking on air' or 'out of this world', expressions which denote elevation beyond the mundane realities — elevation, perhaps, into heaven? They often tell themselves, or articulate to others, 'I'm in heaven', without recognizing the full import of what they are saying.

The very subtleties of human relationships, the reading of one another's thoughts, the instinctive trust and understanding, the comradeship in adversity, the mutual memories and hopes, the rapport between old and young, one generation and another — all these are more than an analyst can explain. And when we focus on the individual we can only cry with Hamlet, 'What a piece of work is a man!' 'Man', as John Buchan says,

> 'precariously perched on this rotating scrapheap, yet so much master of it that he could mould it to his transient uses and, while struggling to live, could entertain thoughts and dreams beyond the bounds of time and space! Man so weak and yet so great, the chief handiwork of the Power that had hung the stars in the firmament.'[15]

Applied to animal and human life, we can still, with the poet William Blake, ask of the tiger, 'What immortal hand or eye/Could frame thy fearful symmetry'[16]; we can wonder with the author of Proverbs at the way of an eagle in the air, the mysterious navigational system by which a bird can find its way across the world (*Proverbs 30:19*). Above all, human beings, for all their flaws, assume there is a Maker. Their very uniqueness, as trillions of individuals, is a compelling argument, as is their capacity to speak (what a miracle!), to laugh, to reason and to imagine, to appreciate and to cherish; their courage and forbearance in suffering.

Apart from its intrinsic worth there are four features of human life that hint at heaven.

The first is our capacity to receive inspiration. I am not thinking now of a genius like Mozart but of ordinary people infiltrated by a creative power illuminating, vitalizing and even transforming them.

A leading Scottish churchman, asked why he had given up a career in the law for one in the Church, replied that he had met a Man. He felt chosen and compelled by a power he identified as the risen Lord. John Newton tells of the 'Amazing Grace' of his conversion:

> 'I once was lost, but now am found,
> Was blind, but now I see.'

This grace came not from himself, nor out of the blue, but through the generative power of the New Testament; to him it was clearly the power of Christ or the work of the Holy Spirit.

This happens in many lives. We are rightly sceptical of some who claim to be born-again Christians but seem to lack grace and humility, but many who may make no such claims have known a liberation, a sustaining power in a time of trouble or the kindling of an inner light (as the Quakers would maintain). The point is that, like grace, it is *given* and has no adequate human explanation. From somewhere beyond us we are endowed and enthused — a hint of heaven.

The second feature is the experience of being guided. With hindsight we see that we were deflected from a wrong course and steered into the right one. From the trace left by the ship, as it were, we discover where we have come from and where we are heading, although we had been unaware of any purpose or pattern at all. Perhaps this is again a hint of heaven.

The third feature I have referred to already when I wrote about love. It is love plus all the other Christian virtues; those listed by St Paul as 'the harvest of the Spirit' (*Galatians 5:22-23*). They are indications of the divine or, in the words of Hebrews 6:5, 'the powers of the age to come'. And since Christians have no monopoly of them, goodness, humility, compassion and the rest are equally signs of heaven. Since human nature is not as has often been misbelieved, fundamentally corrupt, but made in God's image and flawed, there are glimpses of the eternal in all of us. That is why many of us echo St Augustine's words, 'Lord, thou hast made us for thyself and our hearts are restless till they find rest in thee.'[17]

A fourth hint of heaven for those who have eyes to see and ears to hear is found in our desire to make sense of life, to find meaning in our existence. 'Thou madest man, he knows not why/he thinks he was not made to die.'[18] If death were no more than the snuffing out of our little candle, all would be pointless vanity. All good things would indeed come to an end. The whole enterprise of civilization would remain unfinished. There would be no ultimate future, no kingdom of God. We could only be no-hopers. Although it is fair to add that many have given up hope and yet find their living worthwhile, so wonderful is this present world, so precious life itself.

I think, for instance, of the actress and author Anne Bancroft, who has written of the afterlife from her understanding as a Buddhist, that 'there is no permanent soul'[19]. There is an ultimate spiritual reality underlying all we perceive but 'I' am no longer 'I' there, and 'you' are no longer 'you'. What we were is not destroyed but rearranged and we are reborn, and perhaps will revisit this world, but in a different way. 'I do not feel a strong need for personal survival', she writes.

> 'The immediate "now" is where transcendence lies. If I can see the wonder of life as well as the suffering — just the ordinary wonder of stars and clouds, cats and babies — I feel close to the edge of transcendence. Existence is a profound mystery and marvelling at it seems to bring its sacred nature closer. Life after death has little meaning for me, compared with the infinite and miraculous reality of the moment.'[20]

That Anne Bancroft and many like her rejoice and marvel can only be good news. Yet I wonder how they cope with bereavement. For them, the parting must always be a devastating goodbye, never *au revoir*.

Again, if our lives are not given meaning by an afterlife it becomes easier to accept the view that the State is all-important and the individual expendable. 'Where there is not general belief in immortality', wrote P. T. Forsyth, 'the individual withers and the State is more and more'[21] — words written early this century which history has endorsed again and again. When, in 1989, an atheistic Chinese government set its tanks on peacefully protesting students in Tiananmen Square, their disregard for the sanctity of human life was the corollary of their disbelief. The inhumanities of the Third Reich and the Russian government's ruthless treatment of the dissident Chechens in 1994 drive home the point. Before we become complacent, we should also remember the less than Christian treatment of asylum seekers and the homeless in our own country.

'If I am to be extinguished at seventy', Forsyth goes on to say, 'I need not be too concerned about my soul's perfection, to say nothing about being perfect as God is.'[22] True, we ought not to be over-concerned about our own souls but concerned, rather, to be able to contribute to the welfare of our generation and the world we will pass on to our children. The fact remains that if we know we belong to God and have a purpose to fulfil, a vocation and not just a career, we find a sense of dignity and our striving is worthwhile. We are pilgrims on the way, not vagabonds wandering here and there and destined never to reach home.

To those who believe in a divine purpose and have found their vocation, whether it is high or humble, and delight in following it, there is often given not just a hint of heaven but its genuine likeness. This may only mean that they had been his associates but, as so often in Scripture there is a double meaning — they had been with Jesus so intimately that the risen Christ was revealed in them.

Many of us have met people so close to God that their very appearance is numinous. Something as elusive yet as real as the Mona Lisa's smile and far more beautiful — a touch of heaven — is there. When Dr Archie Craig, for instance, visited the Scottish missionary James Graham of Kalimpong, his face struck him as 'a love letter to the human race'.[23]

The old saying that 'a saint is one whom the light shines through' is true; and since the Spirit moves where he will, that light can be seen not only in the faces of Christian believers but also in those of other faiths and of none. It is the clearest hint, and even an incarnation, of heaven. As Robert Browning says in his poem 'The Ring and the Book',

> Through such souls alone
> God stooping shows sufficient of His light
> For us i' the dark to rise by, And I rise.

1. T. S. Eliot, *The Complete Poems and Plays* (London: Faber & Faber, 1969) p. 190
2. William Shakespeare, *Hamlet*, Act 3 Scene 1
3. Robert Vaughan, 'The Retreat'
4. T. S. Eliot, *op.cit.*, p. 272
5. Philip Callow, *Van Gogh: A Life* (London: Allison & Busby, 1969) p. 220
6. Simone Weil, *Waiting on God* (Fontana, 1959) p. 127
7. R. S. Thomas, *Collected Poems* (London: J. M. Dent, 1993) p. 436
8. John McGrath, *The Long Roads* (BBC, 1993)
9. John Baillie, *And the Life Everlasting* (Oxford University Press, 1934) p. 245
10. C. S. Lewis, *Transposition and other Addresses* (London: Geoffrey Bles, 1934) p. 24
11. Bernard Shaw, *St Joan* (Penguin) Scenes 2 and 5
12. Donnie Munro (University of Edinburgh *Student* magazine, October 1994)
13. T. S. Eliot, *Murder in the Cathedral* (Faber & Faber) p. 246
14. Iris Murdoch, *The Black Prince* (Grantham: Chatto & Windus, 1973)
15. John Buchan, *Sick Heart River* (London: Hodder & Stoughton, 1941) p. 195
16. William Blake, 'The Tyger'
17. St Augustine: *Confessions*, Book 1
18. Alfred, Lord Tennyson, 'In Memoriam' (Everyman, 1991)
19. Anne Bancroft interviewed in the *Independent* (1 February 1992)
20. *Ibid.*
21. P. T. Forsyth (1848-1921), *This Life and the Next* (London: MacMillan, 1918)
22. *Ibid.*
23. Elizabeth Templeton, *God's February: A life of Archie Craig* (British Council of Churches) p. 53

3

Seeing and hearing

*'If the doors of perception were cleansed
everything would appear as it is, infinite.'*
William Blake[1]

Premonitions of glory, 'a rumour of angels' — is that all we can be
given? According to Plato we can only see, as it were, shadows
flickering on the wall of a cave; to St Paul, they were the blurred reflections in a mirror (*1 Corinthians 13:12*). When the apostle turns
again to the mirror analogy, however, it is to tell us that Jesus is the
mirror-image of God, the clearest picture of God and therefore of
heaven (*Colossians 1:15*). Apart from this there is only guesswork, for
heaven lies beyond our apprehension.

It is dangerous to guess; for we can only conceive of heaven in an-
thropomorphic terms, measuring what is divine by human standards.
Colleen McDannell and Bernhard Lang, in *Heaven: A History* describe how different generations, cultures, religions, and even social
classes have done just that, each one tending to project its own priori-
ties and desires[2]. It may not be possible to avoid this, but at least we
can keep reminding ourselves of the distance between our guesses and
the transcendent reality; and make sure that the guesses are founded
on our knowledge of God.

Even then we shall be hampered by lack of words. 'The highest cannot be spoken', and for the profoundest mysteries our linguistic and
conceptual tools are inadequate.

And yet we can hazard some guesses based upon what we know of
the Creator. We know the diversity and fecundity of his creation and
can guess that heaven contains no less and presumably even more of

his handiwork. God made the natural world but consider the attention that He has lavished on, for example, the variety of trees, and on every other created thing. I was astonished, for instance, when a collector showed me the variety of grasses in my own back lane.

In a well-researched American novel an agent of the FBI goes to the Smithsonian Institute in Washington to try to identify a chrysalis found on a corpse. It is, says the expert, of the order called Lepidoptera. But he adds that this is a big family of some 30,000 butterflies and 130,000 moths.[3] The breathtaking prodigality of creation! Try to match two pebbles on a beach, or even two human beings, and you will fail. No identical twins are wholly identical, however hard to tell apart.

Until the nineteenth century our ancestors were only dimly aware of the glories of the natural world. It needed painters such as Turner and Constable, the Lakeland poets and Byron, the novelists Sir Walter Scott, Robert Louis Stevenson, Thomas Hardy and many more to open their eyes. Today, however, many people have been encouraged to see by the conservationists: the National Trust, for instance, with its preservation of areas of beauty, and those vigilant environmentalists who resist the vandalising of the countryside. But our chief mentors have been the scientists, notably biologists and botanists like Sir David Attenborough and Dr David Bellamy who, through advances in technology and their communication skills, have revealed to us the marvels of creation. In our homes, thanks to time-lapse photography, they can show us within seconds the lifespan of a flower from its seeding to its blossoming.

It is the scientists, not the cameras, who are the visionaries. In the Introduction to the book of his television series *Life on Earth*, Attenborough makes an illuminating remark. Of his first visit to the tropics he says, 'I remember finding a prodigality of pattern and colour for which I was unprepared, a revelation of the splendour and fecundity of the natural world from which I have never recovered.'[4] Countless Europeans in the tropics have only been aware of the exotic and humid jungle. But the scientists are saying to us, those who have eyes to see, let them see.

And what shall we see? From moonshot to amoeba, we shall see the work of a sublime artist and designer, architect and engineer, colourist and creator who can only be called God. (Yes, there is also in nature the predatory element, cruelty and death, but these no more nullify its wonders than evil negates the marvellous attributes of human nature.) If we can glimpse such a God in the created world we can guess that this is only a hint of his powers, and of heaven.

If the glorious diversity as well as the beauty of the world are hall-marks of heaven, so also is colour. A heaven in monochrome, whether it is a place or not, seems inconceivable. The divine artist who uses such a rich palette on this world, from morning skies to the ladybird's wings, will use an even richer one in the world to come. I am sur-prised that hardly anyone has mentioned this. The Bible mentions only a few symbolic colours: the saints are robed in white and there is scarlet and gold — but we could guess further than this.

And then music, for we must hear as well as see. A silent afterlife, or one broken only by speech, is inconceivable. For those with the gift of music, heaven's bliss would be sorely marred by its absence. Since music is the purest, most unalloyed of the arts, many are convinced that it is a direct link to God. As early as the twelfth century St Hildegard of Bingen, and probably St Cecilia before her, declared that music links human beings with God. For worshippers of Mozart this would not seem an extravagant claim. In a semi-autobiographical novel, William McIlvanney muses, 'Dear W. A. Mozart, What does it feel like to take down God's dictation?'[5] Words echoed by the tenor Luciano Pavarotti who said in an interview, 'I don't think Mozart was a composer. I think Mozart was a carrier, a messenger from God, sent here with music already written.'[6]

Mozart does not stand alone, for all truly great music sounds as if it sprang fully-formed from the composer's pen. Then there is the expe-rience of Handel during those twenty-four days of miraculous inspi-ration when he worked at fever-pitch on the *Messiah*. 'He had by some extraordinary mental feat drawn himself completely out of the world,' wrote the musicologist Newman Flower, 'so that he dwelt — or believed he dwelt — in the pastures of God.'[7] And when he com-pleted the Hallelujah Chorus and finally laid down his pen he said, with tears streaming down his face, 'I did think I did see all Heaven before me, and the great God Himself.'[8]

Then there is Elgar, who professed that he plucked his music from the air, as if to assert that it came from heaven, and whose religious devotion inspired so much of his earlier music. (Sadly, like van Gogh, he was later to lose his faith though not his inspiration.) At the close of *The Dream of Gerontius* his music matched Newman's vision of eternity. Nor is it surprising that when the conductor Sir Malcolm Sargent sent the young Prince Charles recordings of some cello con-certos he commended in particular the slow movement and ending of the Elgar concerto as being 'beyond this world'.[9]

Some people may find the more radical recent composers too

inaccessible to be uplifting. Following Elgar and Fauré, however, there are Benjamin Britten with his *War Requiem* and *Te Deum*, and also Olivier Messiaen; and now, towards the close of the century, there is a spiritual stirring as composers such as John Tavener and Arvo Pärt emerge. Their Scottish counterpart, James Macmillan, affirmed in a broadcast interview in 1994 that it was the composer's responsibility to open up the hidden and the divine.[10]

Other forms of music can raise people into the transcendent, to a (usually unrecognized) experience of God. Among these are the religious works of Bach, the vespers and motets of Monteverdi and Palestrina, Gregorian chant, African American spirituals, and oratorios.

Nor must we forget the music of the masses. At Wembley, Anfield and Twickenham the crowds sing 'Abide with Me', 'You'll Never Walk Alone' and 'Swing Low, Sweet Chariot'. The hints of heaven in the words may pass them by, but the composers' awareness is reflected in their music, and it may be these overtones that have caused such songs to prevail over more mundane anthems. Similarly, Gregorian chants appear in the popular charts and the prayerful music of both the Taizé and the Iona Community is attractive to many.

Creative works do not have to be religiously motivated, and perhaps our thinking about the music of heaven is too restricted. The sacred music of St John's visions on Patmos, described in the Book of Revelation — anthems of praise, performed on a vast scale — is not the whole story. Others may think along the lines of Axel Munthe. In *The Story of San Michele* he recounts a dream in which he confronted the Angel of Death. 'Shall I ever hear again', he heard himself say, 'the sounds of Mozart's Requiem, my beloved Schubert and the titan chords of Beethoven?' The Angel replied: 'It is only an echo from Heaven you overheard.' Likewise, when he confided to the Angel, 'I wish a friendly voice could read the *Phaedo* to me once more', he was told 'The voice was mortal, the words are immortal, you will hear them again.'[11]

But Munthe is too restrictive in thinking only of Mozart, Schubert and Beethoven. My guess is that in the life to come the range of music, like that of colour, will surpass the richness of the earthly one, and that those whose love of music is omnivorous will not be disappointed.

One cannot go further without running into insoluble difficulties. Music as we know it is vocal or instrumental. Does the spiritual body have vocal chords? The next life, according to St Paul, is an embodied life in which we will be able to communicate with our Lord, and surely with one another, but new ways of communication will not necessarily eliminate speech. 'The sound of a voice that is still'[12] is too precious, I believe, to be silenced. And if we can speak we can sing.

Music has always been associated with heaven. Paintings of the Madonna often depict litttle cherubs floating around her carrying a lute or viol, a harp or a miniature pipe-organ in their chubby hands — symbols of the music of heaven.

And there will be music there, for God will not withdraw so divine a gift. And there will be music-makers, for unless they use their gift it will waste away. On earth they are communicators, channels between the composers and listeners; and I cannot think that it will be any different in heaven. Only with this human element is the musical experience possible, so there is no need for music that is given to us, as it were, prepackaged and perfect; or works of art that are flawless, finished works of God; or every person to be a paragon. If this were so, there would be nothing left to strive for. No, the destiny of music, like our own, is not instant perfection but the pursuit of it, the going on from glory to further glory.

In our human weakness we shall probably go on guessing about such things, perhaps in too concrete terms. And yet it may be that heaven is not as immaterial as we fear. As we are resurrected into a new body, there may also be a re-embodiment of the good and innocent pleasures of this life, no longer subject to transience and decay but brought to a new potential so that they are better than we can ever imagine.

This seems to be what Jesus inferred when he promised, 'Your joy shall be made full' (*John 16:24*). All true joy is of heaven, and it is not something different we shall be given there, but the same in fuller measure. 'On the earth the broken arcs', wrote Browning, 'in heaven, a perfect round.'[13] 'The true joy of a good soul in this world', says John Donne, 'is the very joy of heaven; and we go thither not that we might have joy infused into us but that as Christ says, our joy might be full ... for, as he promises that no man shall take away our joy from us, so neither shall death itself take it away, nor so much as interrupt it, or discontinue it ... I shall have a joy, which shall no more evaporate than my soul shall evaporate, a joy that shall pass up, and put on a more glorious garment above and be joy super-invested in glory.'[14]

And it is not too much to suppose that the greatest earthly joys will be reproduced in heaven, and that the dead even now share with us in our joys as they share in our sorrows.

As C. S. Lewis says: 'The new earth and sky, the same yet not the same as these, will rise in us as we have risen in Christ. And once again ... the birds will sing out and the waters flow, and lights and shadows move across the hills and the faces of our friends laugh upon us with amazed recognition.

Guesses, of course, only guesses. If they are not true, something better will be. For we know that we shall be made like Him, for we shall see Him as He is.'[15]

1. William Blake, *The Marriage of Heaven and Hell* (c. 1790-3)
2. Colleen McDannell and Bernhard Lang, *Heaven: A History* (Yale University Press, 1990)
3. Thomas Harris, *The Silence of the Lambs* (London: Reed, 1989)
4. David Attenborough, *Life on Earth* (London: HarperCollins, 1979)
5. William McIlvanney, *The Kiln* (London: Hodder & Stoughton, 1996) p. 154
6. The *Times* (13 July 1991)
7. Newman Flower, *George Frideric Handel* (London: Cassell, 1926) p. 262
8. *Ibid.*, p. 262
9. Charles Reid, *Malcolm Sargent: A Biography* (London: Hodder & Stoughton, 1973)
10. James Macmillan, BBC broadcast, 1994
11. Axel Munthe, *The Story of San Michele* (London: John Murray, 1929) p. 349
12. Alfred, Lord Tennyson, 'The Bridesmaid' (1830)
13. Robert Browning, 'Abt Vogler'
14. *The Sermons of John Donne*, Vol. VII
15. C. S. Lewis, *Letters to Malcolm* (London: Geoffrey Bles, 1963) p. 158

4

The Old Testament

For here we have no lasting city,
but are looking for the city that is to come.

Hebrews 13:14

Hitherto I have drawn from various sources. I turn now to the Bible and it is necessary to state where I stand with regard to its authority. I do not doubt that many of its authors were inspired and that they heard and expressed the Word of God. But not every utterance of the book itself can be regarded as His voice.

You may speak of an inspired composer or musician: you cannot speak of an inspired piano! Nor is there any such thing as an inspired library, only inspired writers and, among historical and biographical works, characters who are inspired. The Bible is a library and not in that sense inspired. Those who claim that it is inerrant and cannot be wrong, and who swallow it whole are much mistaken. Its pages were written by human beings and, like any other writers, they are fallible and subject to occasional error.

Unfortunately there has recently been a resurgence of this narrow bibliolatry, which makes the Bible something to worship. American fundamentalists with vast material resources have infiltrated both the West and the former communist countries of Eastern Europe in what has been called 'the invasion of the sects'. Many Protestants have relapsed into this crude bibliolatry, attributing to the written word an authority which ought to belong only to Christ. These 'Bible Christians' are not idolaters, for they believe as I do that God was in Christ. But when they require us to give unquestioned authority to the Scriptures as well they are misguided. As a wise minister of my youth used to say, 'God has not given us two props, for our faith needs only one.'

However, Bible, Church and sacraments *are* means of grace, which is altogether different. To Christians in the Salvation Army and the Society of Friends the last two are dispensable. All three, however, are divinely-given means of grace: that is why we call them holy. But they are not to be elevated to the level of the Trinity, whom alone Christians worship.

Believing thus, I am not going to batter the sceptics with proof-texts. They would not accept them merely because they are in the Bible, and neither do I.

The afterlife is an area open to human misunderstanding. When we read in the Bible of a triumphalist heaven where the Almighty, like some human potentate, requires unceasing praise; a final judgement in which, like golfers in a major tournament, we do or do not 'make the cut'; and a hell of vindictive torment, we have to discriminate and ask, How much of this can be true? On the other hand, to talk of heaven is to talk of God, and our thoughts of heaven will be shaped by such knowledge of him as we can glean from the Bible.

Turn, then, to the Old Testament. In the ten centuries or more in which it was written there are only a small number of references to an afterlife. There is some mention of the patriarchs being gathered to their fathers — but perhaps only to join them in sleep. Yet to the Lord God are attributed not the words 'I was...' but 'I *am* the God of Abraham and of Isaac and of Jacob', as if to indicate that these patriarchs are alive and aware.

Elijah was carried to heaven in a chariot and when Elisha prayed that his servant's eyes would be opened, 'The Lord opened the eyes of the servant, and he saw; the mountain was full of horses and chariots of fire all around Elisha' *(2 Kings 6:17)*. There is a militaristic element there as well as the merely contemporary one of chariots, which means little to us today. If the ancients interpreted the supernatural in implausible terms, however, it does not follow that their conviction of divine help was mistaken.

David when he loses his child says: 'I shall go to him, but he will not return to me' *(2 Samuel 12:23)*: but what looks like a promise of reunion may only have meant, 'I shall join him in, but not beyond, death'.

When Saul, with the help of a medium, conjured up the spirit of Samuel he was rebuked for his impiety *(1 Samuel 28)*, but the story is in line with the testimony of modern spiritualism, which many people regard as illegitimate and dubious though not entirely bogus.

Saul, in fact, when he believed that Samuel was not beyond hearing distance, showed a more explicit belief in an afterlife than others in the Old Testament who had a deeper spirituality. Job, for instance, whose trust in God never wavered and whose faithfulness contrasts strongly with Saul's spiritual decline, at first believed that death was eternal sleep:

> ... at rest
> with kings and counsellors of the earth ...
> There the wicked cease from troubling,
> and there the weary are at rest.
> The small and the great are there,
> and the slaves are free from their masters.
>
> *(Job 3:14, 17, 19)*

> Before I go, never to return,
> to the land of gloom and deep darkness.
>
> *(Job 10:21)*

In contrast to this are the marvellous words 'I know that my Redeemer lives' *(Job 19:25)*. Even if the capital R is a Christian interpolation, and a more accurate translation is 'For I know that my vindicator lives', Job goes on to refer to 'my defending counsel, even God himself, whom I shall see with my own eyes' — presumably beyond this life.

And in the end Job says, 'I have spoken of things I have not understood, things too wonderful for me to know', and he tells God, 'I knew you then only by report, but now I see you with my own eyes' *(Job 42:3, 5)*. And we are left wondering whether he can still believe that the God who has vindicated him and is at work behind the mystery of all his creation, will leave him to sleep in Sheol for ever.

Job's pilgrimage brought him to a sense of the abiding presence of God. And, as Professor Edgar Jones remarks,

> 'The very quality of [his] communion with God demands in the continuing revelation of God's purpose the fulfilment of the Resurrection faith ... If after reading the Book of Job we ask "Where do we go from here?" we must answer: "to the foot of the Cross and beyond in the company of the Risen Lord".'[1]

Uniquely, the Book of Daniel speaks unequivocally of the afterlife, at a time when the oppressed Israelites looked only for deliverance in this world and the coming of a righteous kingdom:

> Many of those who sleep in the dust of the earth shall awake, some to everlasting life, and some to shame and everlasting contempt. Those who are wise shall shine like the brightness of the sky, and those who lead many to righteousness, like the stars forever and ever *(Daniel 12:2-3).*

What Daniel says of the Son of Man, of the book of life and (in code) of the destiny of nations being determined in heaven, was to influence another visionary, the author of the Book of Revelation. But his reference to the mysterious fourth man in the fiery furnace is more like the visions of Elisha and beyond our capacity to assess. Again it is no insubstantial dream but a testimony to help from the unseen.

Some of the high points of Hebrew religion are in the Psalms. 'But God will ransom my soul from the power of Sheol'; and again, 'You guide me with your counsel, and afterward you will receive me with honour' *(Psalms 49 and 73)*. When Psalm 116 declares, 'Precious in the sight of the Lord is the death of his faithful ones' *(verse 15)*, it is surely saying that such lives are too precious to end in oblivion. There is no place where the assurance of heaven is clearer than in Psalms 23 and 139. The author of the former knows that a shepherd God is with him even in those dark days when life tumbles in, and in death itself when the light of life departs. The goodness and mercy which have followed him all his days are not his only blessings; there is also the assurance 'and I will dwell in the house [the word can mean "presence"] of the Lord for ever' *(AV)*. Nowhere is the faith of the New Testament more confidently anticipated.

To the writer of Psalm 139 also the everlasting God is an intimate presence, so near and real that life here or hereafter is inconceivable without him:

> Even before a word is on my tongue, O Lord,
> you know it completely ...
> If I ascend to heaven, you are there;
> if I make my bed in Sheol, you are there.
> If I take the wings of the morning
> and settle at the farthest limits of the sea,
> even there your hand shall lead me,
> and your right hand shall hold me fast.

Heaven and Sheol (or Hell) may or may not denote the afterlife; but it is clear in this passage that in the highest realms as well as in the lowest depths of the soul, and even in areas beyond our knowledge (the sea being limitless and mysterious as death to the psalmist) there is no separation from God. Here is a faith similar to St Paul's 'Who shall separate us from the love of Christ?', a faith which says, because we are in him who is eternal our eternity is guaranteed.

There are other passages of great significance in the Old Testament. 'Enoch walked with God; then he was no more, because God took him' *(Genesis 5:24)* has more than a hint of heaven. And, from Isaiah *(40:11)*, 'He will feed his flock like a shepherd; he will gather the lambs in his arms, and carry them in his bosom, and gently lead the mother sheep.' A new and better earth, the promised kingdom; or a prospect of heaven? It could be either, or both.

In the intertestamental period (about 200 BC to AD 100) belief in an afterlife grew stronger. Although in the Apocrypha death is generally equated with eternal rest, belief in an afterlife breaks through in such great passages as chapter 3 of the Wisdom of Solomon (verses 1-9), beginning 'But the souls of the righteous are in the hand of God', and 5:15-16:

> But the righteous live forever, and their reward is with the Lord; the Most High takes care of them. Therefore they will receive a glorious crown and a beautiful diadem from the hand of the Lord, because with his right hand he will cover them, and with his arm he will shield them.

As the Pharisees were to make plain in Jesus' time, and devout Jews do today, Judaism does not lack belief in a resurrection. The Christian misunderstanding that Jewish funerals are dominated by sorrow, with no spark of hope, has been answered by Bishop Hugh Montefiore, who was brought up in the Jewish faith. Writing of his belief in eternal life he declared:

> 'Unlike some of my fellow Christians, I do not base this belief on the death and resurrection of Christ. After all, I believed in eternal life before even I had read the Gospels and known the Lord Jesus — as a Jew, did I not express this belief every time I said Kadeesh for the dead? For the Kadeesh prays that God "will revive the dead and raise them up to life eternal".'[2]

His testimony is endorsed by Rabbi Arye Forta in an article on the Jewish view of the afterlife. 'Both the Bible and the Talmud are intensely practical manuals, and the real importance of belief in a world beyond is that it provides a context for life in this one.' He also cites Jacob's reply to Pharaoh's query 'How old are you?' 'The period of my sojourn is ...' as an example of 'the Jewish vision of life sandwiched between a coming from, and a returning to, another plane of existence'. As for heaven, it 'is thought of in terms of closeness to God: "The righteous sit and delight in the radiance of God's presence", says the Talmud.'[3]

When all is said, however, the main contribution of the Old Testament and Judaism to belief in the hereafter is to be found in reading between the lines. In the Old Testament God is forgiving and gracious. The gravity of sin is met with the generosity of God. But were there no afterlife neither sin nor forgiveness would greatly matter.

Again, God is revealed as a God who reaches out to his people and chooses Israel. He binds them to himself by a covenant — 'You will be my people and I will be your God' — and raises up prophets and leaders to prepare them to carry out his will on earth and to bear witness, in a world of false gods, to the one true God.

These dominant themes of covenant and election assume the existence of heaven, for without it such language would be meaningless. Unfortunately, the whole concept of election has been crudely distorted (whether by Calvin or the misunderstanding of Calvin) into an appalling picture of some people being elected from their birth for heaven and others for hell. But God does not select like that. I believe that he calls or elects us all to fulfil a purpose in life; and some are called to bear a special witness and to fulfil a special destiny.

Those, in the Old Testament and beyond, who believed in such a destiny cannot also have believed that it would end with their or their successors' mortality. If it is true that our lives, and the life of the world, have a purpose and a meaning, then we are not merely creatures of a day and our life here is only a sojourn as the people of the Old Testament well knew.

1. Edgar Jones, *The Triumph of Job* (London: SCM Press, 1966) p. 118
2. In the quarterly *Christian* magazine (Easter 1978)
3. Rabbi Árye Forta, The *Independent* (22 February 1992)

5

The New Testament

'He who looks with faith to Jesus is as sure of
the life everlasting as of the forgiveness of sins.'

H. R. Mackintosh[1]

The theme of the New Testament is salvation; the salvation of men and women and the redemption of the world through the coming, death and resurrection of Jesus Christ. And this demands as its corollary an afterlife. If there is no afterlife, what's the point of being saved?

And what are we to make of Jesus? For whether you worship him or only admire him, call him prophet or genius, reformer or Saviour, you have to acknowledge that his life was 'hid with God': he was a man of prayer. He prayed often and taught his disciples to do so. But if there is no God out there and no heaven his life would be founded on an illusion. That he clearly believed in a God 'out there' is sufficient argument against the 'Sea of Faith' theologians who believe only in a God within.

Jesus' own faith points us to heaven. And the recurring theme of his faith is found in the word Father. 'Our Father', 'my Father', 'my Father in heaven', 'your heavenly Father' or simply 'your Father' were constantly on his lips. You cannot accept Jesus only as 'the man for others' and ignore all he says about the Father. He is Father-proclaiming, Father-loving and, if you like, Father-intoxicated as well.

Unless he was entirely deluded and the authority given him, as he claimed, by his Father non-existent, we can postulate an afterlife on this alone. He who with his last breath said, 'Father, into your hands I commend my spirit' *(Luke 23:46)* never doubted it.

People can be so shortsighted that some of us will say, 'I am a Christian but I don't believe in an afterlife.' But this is absurdly illogical: to believe in a man of such faith and yet to reject his faith. Jesus said little directly about the afterlife, but it underlies all his teaching, a subliminal element for those who have ears to hear.

For instance, you can look at the parable of the prodigal son *(Luke 15:11-32)* on two levels. It is a story of forgiveness, restoration and undiminished love, in which we are told of the graciousness of God and of how he wants us to act towards sinners. On this level it closely parallels Hosea where the prophet forgives his errant wife and God speaks of his love for errant Israel. 'O Israel, return to the Lord' *(14:1)*. On the subliminal level the parable tells us that there is joy in heaven over one sinner who repents: thus will our heavenly Father welcome us reprobates home and give us, above all that we deserve, a place at his table.

Again, in the parable of the talents *(Luke 19:12-26)* there are two levels. On the surface it is about our possessions and how we use or fail to use them: but it is also about a time of reckoning and of judgement, and our responsibility before God.

In the parables of the weeds and the net full of fish *(Matthew 13)* Jesus used the metaphor of a harvest. The fruits of field and sea will be gathered in and the good separated from the bad. Wheat is not left to rot or to be burned. The good will survive beyond the harvest. The farmer has a purpose for it; and the farmer is God. It is he who will intervene and bring history to an end; not human beings by some act of nuclear destruction or despoiling of the earth. And that divine purpose must be the extension or renewal of life either in a heaven on earth or a heaven beyond it.

Another parable, that of the rich man and Lazarus *(Luke 16:19-31)*, would seem to have a more direct bearing on the afterlife. Some have cited it as an explicit revelation of a two-tier afterlife in which some reside in glory and others in torment, with a great chasm fixed between them. But the story is a folk-tale, a fable well-known to the Pharisees who had failed to apply it to themselves. The point was the assumption by the rich and powerful that their status was God-given and eternally secure and that the poor and infirm were destined to remain so; and, indeed, were non-persons.

To Jesus the thrust of the story is the relationship of the rich man to Lazarus. He acknowledged no relationship; he was completely indifferent. We, or the Pharisees, may do no deliberate harm to our suffering neighbours whether they are at our gate or in the Third

World; but unless we reach out to them in some way our complacency will be painfully shattered in heaven. We need not take the eternal torment of the rich man literally to understand this. The flames of hell are symbolic, for fire consumes: no-one can survive it for minutes let alone for eternity. What is real is the inner pain. We are told nothing about the equipment of heaven and hell, only about the agony and the ecstasy.

There are more direct sayings. 'I am going to the Father' *(John 14:12)* and 'In my Father's house there are many dwelling places' *(John 14:2)*, for example. Confronted with these, Christ's followers had three options: to believe that he was deluded, or that the words had been put into his mouth, or to accept them. To accept such claims, amplified by John's statement that Jesus was aware 'that he had come from God and was going back to God' *(John 13:3)*, was to court the charge of blasphemy and put their heads on the block, but they did exactly that.

We may not always have the actual words of Jesus, but there are sayings that are too startling and profound to be written off or attributed to his disciples; words which carry his unmistakable authority. There is the reply, for instance, to those who asked if they should pay the Roman tax *(Matthew 21:15-22)*, 'Render unto Caesar ... and unto God...'. That reply authenticates heaven, for as the coin for the tax is engraved with Caesar's image so are we stamped with the image of God and of especial worth to him. To discard us at death, then, would be as nonsensical as someone throwing their wealth — or God his children — into the sea. Or as meaningless as saying that mourners will be comforted, if there is no afterlife and no consolation.

More explicit is what Jesus says to Nathanael: 'You will see heaven opened and the angels of God ascending and descending upon the Son of Man' *(John 1:51)*. Using the analogy of Jacob's dream he speaks of himself as the stairway to heaven, the meeting place of heaven and earth. And is this not the essential message of the New Testament regarding the afterlife — that Jesus is the way? The Christian belief is founded basically not on what the Bible says nor on any sayings or incidents it records but on the person of Christ. Once we have encountered God in him, in the historic Jesus or in Jesus met in some upper room, some place of worship, or out on the Emmaus road today when we are about our business and not expecting him, or in someone whose life is possessed by his spirit, which we call the Holy Spirit; then the question, Is there an afterlife? is answered.

To attempt to cover all the apposite New Testament texts is not my purpose, because proof-texts are resisted by those who do not believe. On the other hand they have fortified many in bereavement, as witness the enormous popularity of J. Paterson Smyth's *The Gospel of the Hereafter*. For over sixty years this book has been reprinted more often than any other work on the subject; this is where to look if you want to find out more about what the New Testament says.

There are four crucial passages about heaven in the Gospels, namely, Jesus' reply to the question, 'Whose wife will she be in heaven?' *(Mark 12:29)* and the accounts of his Transfiguration, Resurrection and Ascension.

First, 'Whose wife will she be?' The question is based on the compassionate Jewish Law of Levirate marriage whereby a destitute widow, with no social security, became the responsibility of her brother-in-law. If he too died, then, hopefully, there was another brother. The fact that Jesus' questioners, however, cited seven brothers turned what might have been a serious enquiry into a frivolous one. So he deflected their question with the briefest of answers: 'In heaven there is no marriage'.

To many of us, for whom marriage has been the sublimest of God's gifts, this may seem disconcerting; and for those who have had more than one successful marriage, not very illuminating. But what Jesus is saying is not that any deep and true relationship will be broken, but that we are not to think of heaven in earthly terms. Marriage, as the Sadducees perceived it, was a legal arrangement in which a husband owned a wife. It ought to issue in a happy home and a shared delight in the children and the partners should cherish one another, but primarily it was a contract. Regarding heaven, we have to think in other terms. We shall love and be loved and no doubt commit ourselves to one another in unique relationships, but in a different body and without all the elements of legality, money, property and provision that enter into marriage. True affinity is what matters, and that cannot be broken. For love is eternal, 'the foreverness of real love', and God will not take from us the special affection we have for our own and, it may be, for several generations of our families.

Turn now to those three mysterious supernatural events which are pinnacles in the Christian story. They are all oriented towards heaven. At the Transfiguration the veil is opened. At Easter, although he told Mary, 'I have not yet ascended' *(John 20:17)* he had left this world; and perhaps, as Peter later suggested, was about to visit 'the souls of the departed in prison' *(1 Peter 3:19)*, which may mean telling the good news of the gospel to those who had never heard it. At the Ascension, it may not have been to a heaven which is 'up there' that he returned, but it was to the Father, and to the cosmic authority which he had abandoned in order to become fully human.

The highest pinnacle is the cataclysmic event of the Resurrection. It does not belong to a sequence, but stands on its own and I take it first. To Christians it is the supreme vindication of the life to come.

As anyone who reads the Book of Acts can see, the belief that Jesus was raised from the dead was an inspiration to the Church in a hostile world. Ordinary men and women were possessed with extraordinary courage and became saints and martyrs; and the emblem of cruelty and shame, the cross, became the symbol of salvation. Had Jesus not been raised, as St Paul rightly said, the gospel would have been 'null and void' *(1 Corinthians 15:14)*. Some of Jesus' teaching would have survived — his brokenhearted disciples would at least have seen to that — but the bulk of it would have been discredited. All he had said about faith in God and overcoming the world would be a mockery, the cross a bleak tragedy and the kingdom a delusion.

The New Testament was born out of the faith of the Church. With no Resurrection there would have been no gospel, no faith and probably no Church. Certainly no news of a God who 'visited and redeemed his people', and no power to forgive, comfort and heal, nor to transform either our lives or the world's. Baptism — the promise of new life in Christ — would be meaningless, and Holy Communion only a memorial service. And assurances such as 'I go to prepare a place for you, and I will come again' *(John 14:3)*, indeed every prognostication, whether of his own future, his followers' or the world's, would be the delusions of a half-crazy prophet.

Some believe that Jesus lives on only as a potent influence, but there is no good news of the love of God in that. Humanism may be noble and agnosticism sincere, but they have no gospel. Muslims, Hindus and Jews concede him a place among the prophets without realizing how many elisions they are making in his teaching and how sorely they are abridging his life.

It is not the empty tomb that persuades me. It is what St Mark attests in the closing words of his Gospel: 'the Lord worked with them and confirmed the message by the signs that accompanied it' *(Mark 16:20)*. To know his presence and to have seen his miracles, broken lives and broken homes made new, renewed purpose in people who have lost heart and the revival of love and laughter, is to live in the light of the Resurrection.

But what many find hard to swallow is the empty tomb. Frank Morison's *Who Moved the Stone?* examines every theory put forward by those who would set aside the miracle: either it was a myth or, from various motives, this party or that may have removed the body.[2] But even if such detective work is impeccable the enigma remains, both of what happened at the tomb and of the later resurrection appearances; and the attempt to prove any supernatural event set in a pre-scientific age leaves the unbeliever cold.

To believe in miracles requires faith; and those who believe in a God who is the Creator of heaven and earth dare not say that the empty tomb is beyond his power. It is also through faith that the eternal life of Christ and the presence of God are revealed, and this is of more urgency than any consideration of the afterlife. As John Baillie has finely said:

> 'That a man should be doomed to go through this present life without any sense of God's accompanying presence is a much greater tragedy than that he should be faced with the prospect of extinction when at last he dies.'[3]

If Jesus' body had not been resurrected, it would not prove that belief in the Resurrection is wrong; not now, when his living presence has been made known to millions. In the aftermath of Calvary it was different. If his body had remained in the grave then, his followers would have found it harder to believe. This may be why God gave that generation a sign, a divine word in response to those who in killing Jesus thought that theirs was the final one.

The empty tomb is still a sign; that we are not to look back to a grave, nor linger at it, nor venerate ancient bones and turn them into relics, but move on. Go to Galilee, the angel told them (and it could equally be to London or New York or wherever life takes us), and he will meet you there.

The resurrection appearances were also a sign. And they confirm that heaven is not a strange, forbidding country but his Father's house. As Jesus walked and talked with the disciples again, cooked fish and broke bread, he assumed forms familiar to them; but we cannot be certain that these are clues to the afterlife. In whatever form we shall see him, he will be something more than the man from Nazareth —

the exalted, glorified figure of whom the disciples were given a glimpse at his transfiguration.

The Transfiguration: here is another pinnacle *(Luke 9:28-36)*. On that hilltop (traditionally Mount Tabor) Moses and Elijah, long dead, 'appeared unto them' — not only to Jesus but to three disciples as well. It was a lifting of the veil and vindicated what he had always taught, the reality of heaven. And there the patriarchs counselled him on the eve of his passion, confirmed him in his purpose and fortified his spirit.

On Good Friday heaven would be silent, for he had to know the loneliness and dereliction of extreme suffering and sin-bearing; but now there were Moses and Elijah who had themselves borne the burden of God's ungrateful people as Jesus bore the greater burden of the whole world and its sin. They spoke with him of 'his departure' *(Luke 9:31)*, and later at the Last Supper he was to echo this. 'The Son of Man', he said, 'is going as it has been determined' *(Luke 22:22)*. Moses and Elijah brought that message, and they can only have learned it, and about him, in heaven; in their lifetime the Scriptures were not yet written, nor his coming known.

Their appearance bears out several ideas already discussed. In heaven we will retain our identity and keep company with kindred souls, perhaps, as with Moses and Elijah, from entirely different generations. And, as they did, we will enter further into the truth. The unseen world, we note, is not remote but near; a truth contained, but too little grasped, in the doctrine of the communion of saints.

Above all, the Transfiguration gave to the disciples, and gives to us, a foretaste of Christ's heavenly glory, of what he is to all eternity.

The Gospels end and the Acts begins with the Ascension — but what does this mean? People ask whether he was levitated beyond the skies, or whether the cloud that received him was symbolic, representing the glory and, as with Moses, the presence of God.

Levitation cannot be ruled out, for Teresa of Avila and others of exceptional sanctity experienced it. And space travel has shown in our time how, under certain conditions, the body can become weightless. Yet the mode of Christ's going is irrelevant. Ascension denotes up-ness in a deeper sense, as you might say 'I look up to you' while addressing someone physically smaller than yourself. 'Up to heaven' is not a geographical indication. He is above us through his ascendancy, because at the Ascension his ministry was no longer confined to Galilee and Judaea but extended to the ends of the earth and to the end of time, and because he is Lord of all. And wherever we go he is there, waiting to surprise us.

He still visits us but his dwelling-place is not here. He ascended into heaven taking with him our humanity in which he had shared. We will find that heaven therefore is humanity's goal and final resting place; it is not a realm of alien spirits but of all that is truly and familiarly human.

Christ's ascendancy is also over the powers of evil, the divine yes to their no; it vindicates the victory of the cross, and the promise that the kingdoms of the world will one day be the kingdom of our God and of his Christ. And what it says about heaven is that he is there as king of kings and lord of lords. Meanwhile, here and now, we are to ascend with him by lifting up our hearts and minds to heaven: which, above all, is what I want to say in this book.

Apart from the Gospels, St Paul and the St John of the Book of Revelation are the prime New Testament sources, though the letters of Peter and John should not be overlooked (e.g. 1 Peter 1:4; 3:18-22; 4:13; 5:10-11; 1 John 1:1-7). And the eleventh chapter of Hebrews, which honours men and women of faith, a faith which clearly looks beyond this world. Abraham 'looked forward to the city that has foundations, whose architect and builder is God' *(v.10)*. And of all who died in faith the writer says that 'they confessed that they were strangers and foreigners on the earth ... they desire a better country, that is, a heavenly one. Therefore God is not ashamed to be called their God; indeed he has prepared a city for them' *(vs 13 and 16)*.

Above all, in Hebrews, Jesus is exalted in heaven. He is no longer 'made lower than the angels', but receives glory and honour at his Father's side. He is compared to the high priest who entered the holy place of God, 'the inner shrine behind the curtain where [he], a forerunner on our behalf, has entered, having become a high priest forever' *(6:19-20)*.

St Paul, although he asserts that 'flesh and blood can never possess the kingdom of God' *(1 Corinthians 15)*, sees the afterlife as an embodied life. In the great chapter on life after death he speaks of the natural or physical body being raised as a spiritual body. And in 2 Corinthians 5, using the analogy of a tent (our earthly body) being dismantled and an eternal house provided, he envisages this as 'a heavenly frame' for the spirit.

But the most important thing St Paul has to say is that on the Damascus road he was confronted by Christ, and came to know that

Christ dwelt in him. Consequently he believed that to die was to be with Christ and to see him no longer 'in a mirror dimly' but face to face. But might not the blinding vision and the voice he heard have been hallucinations, the result of sunstroke compounded with his inner torment? 'Critics', my father once wrote in a study of St Paul,

> 'theorize on the assumption that intense beliefs may produce visions. In the main that is correct, but they overlook the important fact that in Paul's case it was not intense belief that produced the vision, but the vision that produced the intense belief.'[4]

He was given it because he was chosen by God so that his life might be the clearest of all signs to the truth of the Resurrection.

St Paul gets to the very heart of the matter in 1 Corinthians 15:16: 'If the dead are not raised, then Christ has not been raised. If Christ has not been raised, your faith is futile.' But he is wise enough, as J. S. Stewart says, 'not to frame a fully articulated scheme of eschatology ... The apostle's dreams of the future, his sudden insights, his flashes of vision, his long deep ponderings and meditations, are not patient of such treatment'.[5]

And confident as he is of heaven, St Paul is conscious of how little — and yet how much — we know of it. Quoting from Isaiah he refers to 'what no eye has seen, nor ear heard, nor the human heart conceived, what God has prepared for those who love him'; but adds that 'these things God has revealed to us through the Spirit' (1 Corinthians 2:9-10). To say that we know nothing of heaven is not true: foretastes are given us. It is because I go along with St Paul in this that I have been able to write this book.

Much more could be quoted from St Paul. His letters are full of nuggets too precious to ignore but too numerous to spell out (e.g. Romans 6:5-9, 8:18, 38, 39; 1 Corinthians 2:9, 13:12; Ephesians 1:11-14; Philippians 3:10-1;Colossians 1:4-5, 3:1-3).

We pass on to the strange, cryptic Book of the Revelation, with its bizarre images. Much of its symbolism comes from Jewish apocalyptic literature and is reminiscent of passages in Daniel, Ezekiel and the Apocrypha; and we are not expected to take literally the throne, the eyes of flame and hair like wool, the extraordinary beasts, the Lamb on the throne, the precisely numbered saints and warriors, and the precious stones. Many of the symbolic passages were addressed to the condition of the persecuted Church of the first century and some, like the letters to the seven churches *(Revelation 2 and 3)*, still speak to ours. But it is when St John says, 'and his servants will worship him; they will see his face, and his name will be on their foreheads' that we recognize a true disclosure of heaven. When he speaks of 'the marriage supper of the Lamb' *(Revelation 19:9)*, describes an hour of victory when the forces of darkness are overthrown, and foretells that 'Death will be no more; mourning and crying and pain will be no more'*(Revelation 21:4)*, when the old pain-filled earth is done away and there is no longer cause to weep over Jerusalem it is an authentic word. The end of history's long story could not be other than this if God is Alpha and Omega, the first and the last *(Revelation 22:12)*.

Like everyone else, St John can only give us hints and guesses. What is heaven like? Well, he says, there will be no temple and no more sea. But these are not hard facts. Elsewhere there are eight or nine references to a temple where the martyrs serve God day and night. And 'no more sea' may only be a symbol of separation — or the prejudice of a landlubber to whom it denoted unfathomable mystery and unknown terrors. The inconsistencies, the symbols open to various interpretations and the borrowings from Jewish mysticism should make us extremely cautious about drawing literal conclusions.

The overall vision is inspiring. But we need to remember, as H. R. Mackintosh stresses in his classic *The Person of Jesus Christ*, that the central message of Revelation is not about heaven but about Christ.[6] It is the most Christocentric of books. In it Jesus is glorified and is at God's right hand. The crucified one conquers and judges, comforts and reigns together with Almighty God.

If this is the truth about heaven — that before Christ every knee shall bow and that the multitudes who praise him belong to all races, nations and tongues — then there are enormous implications for the human family. Heaven is not for the elect, or an élite, but for all people everywhere. Nor is there a Jewish, Muslim or Buddhist heaven from which Christ is absent. All faiths when followed sincerely bring men and women to God. Yet, if St John is right and Christ is lord of all, the Jew, the Muslim and the Buddhist, all dear to the Father and not to be spurned from his heaven, will confront him there and know that he is, for them also, the way, the truth and the life.

The good news is that Christ died for all, both the living and the dead. And so we celebrate his death in the Eucharist, the feast he instituted which, whatever else it may be, is an eschatological banquet or prefiguring of the afterlife; the last great New Testament sign which both looks forward 'until he come' and is the prototype of a Eucharist in heaven, when with our Saviour we shall continue to celebrate our own and the world's salvation.

The Eucharist is also associated with the idea of a covenant. 'This is my blood of the covenant,' said Jesus as he took the cup *(Mark 14:24)*. The word 'covenant', conspicuous in the Old Testament, was familiar to those who heard Jesus. They would think of the promise or covenant in Jeremiah 31:33f.: 'I will put my law within them and I will write it on their hearts; and I will be their God ... for they shall all know me, from the least of them to the greatest.' But this would be an empty promise unless Christ is alive to fulfil it and there is an unseen world, a heaven, around us.

The good news of the New Testament (or New Covenant) is that God loves us and calls us to serve him. This carries implications for eternity. He is not going to go so far and then abandon us when we die. What the New Testament says I have summarized in one chapter. Were I asked to encapsulate it in just one verse, it would have to be John 3:16: 'For God so loved the world that he gave his only Son, so that everyone who believes in him may not perish but may have eternal life.' The New Testament is about the love which gave us Jesus Christ and the further gift — through him — of eternal life, which is both now and for keeps, a foretaste of the life everlasting.

1. H. R. Mackintosh (1870-1936), *Immortality and the Future* (London: Hodder & Stoughton, 1915) closing words
2. Frank Morison, *Who Moved the Stone?* (Faber & Faber, 1930)
3. John Baillie, *And the Life Everlasting* (Oxford University Press, 1934) p. 159
4. Leon Levison, *Life of St Paul* (Marshall Bros., 1918) p. 28
5. J. S. Stewart, *A Man in Christ* (London: Hodder & Stoughton, 1935) p. 266
6. H. R. Mackintosh, *The Person of Jesus Christ* (Edinburgh: T. & T. Clark, 1912)

6

The harsh sayings

*'In a universe of love there can be no heaven which
tolerates a chamber of horrors, no hell for any which
does not at the same time make it hell for God.'*

Bishop J. A. T. Robinson[1]

Chapter 25 of St Matthew's Gospel pulls no punches. First, there is the ending of the parable of the ten bridesmaids: 'Sir, sir! Let us in!' they cried. But he answered, 'Certainly not! I don't know you.' Then follows the parable of the talents or coins: 'As for this useless servant, throw him outside in the darkness; there he will cry and grind his teeth.' Then comes the picture of the Last Judgement: '"Whenever you refused to help one of these least important ones, you refused to help me." These, then, will be sent off to eternal punishment, but the righteous will go to eternal life' *(Matthew 25:11/12 and 25:45-6)*.[2]

The interpretation of the corn and the weeds is equally harsh: 'The Son of Man will send out his angels to gather up out of his Kingdom all those who cause people to sin and all others who do evil things, and they will throw them into the fiery furnace, where they will cry and grind their teeth' *(Matthew 13:24-30, 36-43)*.[3]

Divine anger is surely indisputable; it is the only response that a God of righteousness, holiness and love can make to the unspeakable callousness and cruelty of many of his children, to what they do to one another and to his world.

But eternal punishment is something else. It is incompatible with the mind of Christ, and makes no sense. On earth we punish those who break the law, in order to protect society and as a deterrent. In heaven these motives cannot apply. Nor can we conceive the Father of Jesus Christ as a vindictive God. The harsher predictions must therefore be explained in a way compatible with a Christlike God; two points may help us here.

The first is that some of these 'harsh sayings' are interpolations and not the actual words of Jesus. They are what D. S. Cairns called 'Jewish survivals in Christian minds',[4] echoes of Jewish apocalyptic reflecting the fierce resentment of persecuted believers towards their heathen oppressors and the enemies of their faith.

This could certainly account for those passages which purport to interpret parables. For it was not characteristic of Jesus to offer interpretations: he spoke in parables expressly so that people might search out the meanings for themselves. To explain a parable has been likened to explaining a joke: it is something you should not have to do.

Nevertheless we are left with other threatening and uncompromisingly severe sayings which cannot be accounted for in this way. To interpret these correctly we have to keep something else in mind — Jesus' use of hyperbole or exaggeration.

Even in the prosaic West we are familiar with hyperbole. For us it is primarily the language of poetry and love. Robert Burns, for example, will pursue his beloved 'Till a' the seas gang dry, my dear/And the rocks melt wi' the sun'.[5] When Jesus points to the scarlet anemones and says, 'Even Solomon in all his glory was not clothed like one of these' *(Luke 12:27)*, he reveals the same poetic mind. And as a Jew and a rabbi or teacher, he was accustomed to using picturesque hyperbole.

This heightened mode of speech was, and still is, normal in both the Middle and Far East. When a courtier, for example, said to a Japanese Emperor, 'May His Imperial Highness live for a thousand years', he meant no more than 'Long may you reign'. My father, who emigrated from Galilee to Scotland, retained this characteristic. I recall his warning when he heard that a neighbour's boy had said 'Shut up' to his mother and been soundly beaten for it. 'If you were to do that,' he told my brother and myself, 'I would break every bone in your body.' We didn't take that literally, but it made a lasting impression, even though, or perhaps because, he was the mildest of men.

Examples of Jesus' use of hyperbole abound. 'If your right eye causes you to sin, tear it out' *(Matthew 5:29).*' 'You strain out a gnat but swallow a camel' *(23:24)*. 'Even the hairs of your head are all counted' *(10:30)*. The beam, or plank, in the eye. The camel and the eye of a needle. Unimaginative commentators, wildly theorizing, have identified a 'Needle Gate' in Jerusalem through which the camel might just squeeze; but the saying needs neither that kind of credibility nor to be watered down. Nor is Jesus saying that no rich person can enter the kingdom. He is simply using hyperbole to warn of the dangers of materialism. And when he said of those who harm children, 'It would be better for you if a millstone were hung around your neck and you were thrown into the sea' (Luke 17:2) he was expressing the anger of God rather than hinting at some dire form of retribution.

When Jesus speaks of the devil, of everlasting flames and harsh punishment (although reputable scholars such as Joachim Jeremias and T. W. Manson are doubtful whether such passages belong to the authentic central stratum of the Gospels) he is, surely, employing Hebrew hyperbole. He is certainly using the imagery with which his hearers were familiar, and it vividly conveys the truth of God's condemnation of evil and has to be taken seriously. The possibility, not of flames but of darkness, and the inability to see God or accept his forgiveness remains. Hell is dereliction, a wasteland from which God is absent. Nor is the loveless, selfish, irresponsible life ready for heavenly bliss. Whether or for how long a soul unable to love will remain derelict, or whether it might resist God for ever — these questions have long troubled the Church and we must consider them.

A quotation from the diary of Malcolm Muggeridge sets the scene:

> 'The reconciliation of the idea of a loving God with the idea of eternal torment was one of the most remarkable feats the human mind had ever performed. Hell up to Calvin was mitigated by purgatory and indulgences. After Calvin, it really was presented as the only alternative to salvation, and began to haunt human beings, for instance Bunyan, who was almost driven mad by the fear of Hell buzzing in his ears.'[6]

The fear of hell no longer haunts us, but we cannot face eternity with complacency. In the searching presence of God our souls will be laid bare, and we shall know how feebly we have served him and what wounds we have inflicted on others and on ourselves. There does not have to be a court or judgement: simply meeting a saint judges us. We are judged far more when we enter the presence of God even here on earth; and infinitely more in heaven. Like Peter, when he saw the holiness of Christ, we may cry out, 'Go away from me, Lord, for I am a sinful man!' (Luke 5:8).

We no longer believe in a Recording Angel; that somewhat ludicrous figure with his vast inventory of our achievements and misdeeds. And when the soldier in Studdert Kennedy's poem 'Well?' dreams of his imminent death he finds no record books in heaven and hears no judge's verdict. He sees only the Christ and hears the one word ' — 'Well?'.[7]

Maybe the 'Well?' smacks too much of a school teacher saying to a recalcitrant pupil, 'And what have you been up to?' or, 'What have you to say for yourself?' Maybe the soldier missed something — a twinkle and a kindness in the Judge's eyes. But the poem makes a valid point: our judgement, like Peter's, will include self-awareness and self-accusation. And the setting will not resemble a law court. Indeed the metaphor of a court with a wrongdoer in the dock is unsatisfactory and misleading.

There will not be a law court; but there will be justice. The inequalities of life cry out for it. The afterlife cannot be one in which wrongs are not righted and the wicked get away with their misdeeds. In such sayings as 'Many that are first will be last, and the last will be first'(*Matthew 19:30*), Jesus makes this clear. There will be a redressing of life's ills, for God is just. The concept of rewards and punishments and blessings and deprivations is therefore entirely credible. But not blessings and cursings, for cursings are incompatible with the divine nature (in spite of Jesus' so-called cursing of the barren fig-tree in Matthew 21:19), though the word 'woe' which Jesus applied to certain Pharisees is apt, for it foretells the grief and pain that some must suffer in the world to come.

Of this we can be sure: everlasting punishment is no-one's lot. The monsters of history, who brought suffering and death to millions, such as Nero and Ivan the Terrible, Hitler and Stalin, are either beyond redemption and blotted out or, after much tribulation and penance, will be saved; but only a sadistic deity would demand an eye for an eye or impose infinite torment.

Are all, then, to be saved, apart from those whose souls are dead? Is there, for billions of unbelievers, a second chance? There are those who say no; this life is the sole sphere of salvation and at death we are either saved or doomed. This conclusion of ultra-Calvinist theology is repugnant to those who believe in a God of grace and love. How can those born into a pernicious environment or a faithless and loveless home, and dying prematurely, be judged on opportunities they never had? How can we be saved and others doomed when at their age — and I think of those killed in war — we were as immature or unbelieving as many of them? A theology which flies in the face of justice must, like the law, be an ass.

Not only must there be a second chance for many but further chances of growth for us all, for we pass through death still immature. We are far from ready for the full life of heaven. If we were suddenly made perfect, all our development, our struggle towards betterment would not matter; we would be transformed whether we liked it or not and there would be no continuing pilgrimage.

But if we are still on the way how are we to reconcile this with the scriptural promises of immediate bliss, of being in St Peter's words 'participants of the divine nature' *(2 Peter 1:4)*, of a new life united to Christ? Can we be purged of all selfishness and pride, all lust and greed, all envy and malice, and yet still have room for enrichment, room to grow? The answer must be yes.

But having a second chance and opportunities for amendment and growth could remove all restraints, so that we can take our ease and say with the young St Augustine, 'Give me chastity ... but not yet'.[8] And it could endorse the doctrine of universalism, which sees everyone saved, and the German writer Heinrich Heine's complacent, 'God will forgive me: it is His *métier* to forgive'.[9]

> 'If we decide for universalism', says John Baillie wisely, 'it must be for a form of it which does nothing to decrease the urgency of immediate repentance and which makes no promises to the procrastinating sinner. It is doubtful whether such a form of the doctrine has yet been found.'[10]

The theologians have still to meet this challenge. But surely there is urgency in the gospel itself. It lies not in the fear of hell and the old-time evangelists' warning, 'What will happen to you unless you repent?', nor in Billy Graham's blunt (but taken out of context) threat, 'The soul that sinneth, it shall [surely] die' *(Ezekiel 18:4, 20, AV)*. Our own need and the world's for Christ is urgency enough. Unless we repent now, our potential as parents or citizens or contributors to the common good cannot be achieved. Unless we repent, change direction and turn to God, he cannot give us the full joy of his presence, or enable us to rise above life's ills. Unless we do it now, we will miss opportunities of serving the Church and the world and the cause of Christ will be that much under-supported.

Jesus came not to condemn the world, but that the world might be saved *(John 3:17)*. His gospel is one of hope. Universalism is the belief that heaven is for all, and that all can have hope. In its extreme form it declares that not one soul will be lost, for the grace of God is bound to prevail; in the end no human will can resist him. On the other hand, we have been endowed with the freedom to resist. According to the New Testament, some are consigned to an outer darkness as the consequence of their rejection of the light. To change the metaphor, a nail can become so rusted that it can no longer respond to a magnet. To sin against the Holy Spirit may mean just that, the corrosion of whatever is holy within us: a fearful prospect indeed.

One thing is clear. It is not only an elect, an élite or the 'born-again' Christian who will enter heaven. Jesus made that plain in his attitude towards those whom the Pharisees wrote off as outcasts, most explicitly in his promise to the dying thief *(Luke 23:43)*. And St Paul, who saw more deeply than any of us into the mind of Christ, told the Roman Governor, Felix, 'I have a hope in God — a hope that they themselves [his accusers] also accept — that there will be a resurrection of both the righteous and the unrighteous' *(Acts 24:15)*. And he looked forward also to the day when all Israel would be saved.

Michael Ramsey, a great and devout Archbishop of Canterbury, thought deeply about these things and was convinced that he would meet again in heaven his much-loved brother, who was an atheist but who had such integrity and humanity that a God who is love could not possibly spurn him.

From the time of St John Chrysostom in the fourth century onwards, many theologians have supported universalism. Others have rejected it. For myself I accept it, but with some reservations, recognizing the force of William Temple's words:

> 'God so longs for a freely offered life that He risks the loss involved in a choice which brings perdition. Because He is love, He made us free; because we are free, we may choose to perish. ... The New Testament certainly teaches that on the choice of every will an infinite issue lies. The question at stake is not one of less or more, nor one of sooner or later; it is one of life or death. And it is good for us that it should be so. It is bracing to the will that it should have real responsibility; and of this a dogmatic universalism would deprive it.'[11]

And yet, despite those who may finally resist God, the world is to be redeemed, all things return to their Creator and his kingdom come on an earth renewed. That is why we affirm that 'at the name of Jesus every knee should bend, in heaven and on earth and under the earth, and every tongue should confess that Jesus Christ is Lord' *(Philippians 2:10-11).*

1. J. A. T. Robinson, *In the End, God* (London: James Clarke, 1950) p. 123
2. Scriptures quoted from the *Good News Bible* published by The Bible Societies/HarperCollins Publishers Ltd UK © American Bible Society, 1966, 1971, 1976, 1992
3. *Ibid.*
4. D. S. Cairns, *A System of Christian Doctrine*, compiled by his son David Cairns (Edinburgh: St Andrew Press, 1979) p. 192
5. Robert Burns, 'My Love Is Like A Red, Red Rose'
6. Malcolm Muggeridge, *Like It Was* (London: HarperCollins, 1981) pp. 159-60
7. G. A. Studdert Kennedy, *Rough Rhymes of a Padré* (1918), later published in *The Unutterable Beauty* (London: Hodder & Stoughton, 1941) p. 135
8. St Augustine, *Confessions*, Bk VIII, Ch. 7
9. Heine on his deathbed; see Lombroso, *The Man of Genius* (1891)
10. John Baillie, *And the Life Everlasting* (Oxford University Press, 1934) p. 245
11. William Temple, *Christus Veritas* (London: Macmillan, 1930) p. 209

7

Judgement to come

'The sole possible function of judgement can be to enable men to receive the mercy which renders it superfluous.'

Bishop J. A. T. Robinson[1]

This most difficult aspect of the life to come requires more consideration. We have seen that when we die and are taken into the heavenly realm we confront what is holy and are inevitably judged. But what of the Last Judgement, so clearly foretold in Scripture and the Creeds? Is there to be a judgement of the nations and the world? And where does forgiveness come in: if we are made clean at the beginning, how can we be judged again at the end? Or is there no beginning or ending but, beyond time, what is to be has already been? We may not find answers but we cannot ignore the questions. In the following pages I am greatly indebted to Simon Tugwell OP, whose knowledge of the early Church Fathers and his own wisdom throw much light on this difficult subject.[2]

'God did not send the Son into the world to condemn the world', says St John, 'but in order that the world might be saved through him' (*John 3:17*). But as his death drew near Jesus said, 'Now is the judgement of this world; now the ruler of this world will be driven out. And I, when I am lifted up from the earth, will draw all people to myself' (*John 12:31-32*).

These words mean that the divine judgement does not occur only in the life to come. The crucifixion exposed and condemned the wickedness, weakness and failure both of that age and of every age of humankind. In the light of that glory, revealed at the cross, we are far from holy. The best we can claim is that we are on the way.

Yet when the scenery of our lives is exposed in heaven, as a flare illuminates a landscape, this is not to be feared; for, as St John shows in his First Letter *(1 John 4:17)*, love brings boldness. Moreover, we can never stop at judgement but must always pass on to grace. Our judge, the New Testament affirms, is Christ, his Holy Spirit is our advocate and we will be acquitted. And then we shall continue as *travellers*, people who have not yet arrived, learning more and more of 'the boundless riches of Christ', growing in love and pressing on, in St Paul's words, 'to maturity, to the measure of the full stature of Christ' *(Ephesians 4:13)*.

As the individual comes under judgement so does the world. 'The history of the world is the judgement of the world'[3], said the German poet Friedrich Schiller, and one can see what he meant. Arrogant empires rise and fall and their rottenness is exposed; nations that live by the sword die by the sword; false ideologies crumble while the Church, where it is faithful, survives.

Yes, there is an ongoing judgement. More difficult to understand is how the nations can be judged at the end of time. It may be, of course, that what the early Christians wrote was coloured by their circumstances. Having the misfortune to live under corrupt, pagan and tyrannical rulers, they looked to the Almighty to sort things out. We, with an awareness of the fluctuations of recent history, cannot fail to recognize how volatile nations are. With any change of government their character and their policies may alter from more or less righteous to more or less satanic almost overnight. Nor can a corrupt government taint a whole nation. In Sodom there were ten just men, and for their sake the city was not destroyed *(Genesis 18)*.

So what does the judgement of the nations mean? Surely not a blanket condemnation or acquittal, but according to every people's and each person's measure of opportunity, responsibility and handling of power. At the same time the guilt of our nation is our guilt too. We are involved and like Isaiah have to confess, 'I am a man of unclean lips and I live among a people of unclean lips' *(Isaiah 6:5)*. When, some day, our nation is asked, 'Have you fed the hungry, healed the sick, and cared for those in prison?' the question is also, have we played our part? But the moment of truth, when it comes for us, is not at the end or consummation of all things. We, and the nations, come under God's judgement now; and a Last Judgement seems redundant except for the final generation.

A last day, yes; a day of harvest when this world comes to an end, the corn and weeds are sorted out and only what is true and just, loving and pure will survive. But God being almighty love, it will be an advent or coming of love: and though the weeds of evil will suffer the anger of God there will be for many a blessed denouement rather than a day of wrath. Fauré, alone among the great composers, seems to have appreciated this when he omitted the usual *Dies Irae* ('Day of Wrath') section from his Requiem.

Yet difficult questions arise, similar to those concerning the characters of nations. 'When the Son of Man comes in his glory', says St Matthew, '... he will separate people one from another, as a shepherd separates the sheep from the goats' *(Matthew 25:32)*. But this is too simplistic. It is only in melodrama or unsophisticated Western films that the 'goodies' are so sharply distinguished from the 'baddies'. The reality is more complex. There are dark places in the lives of essentially decent people and redeeming features in the depraved.

I suggest that here again Jesus is using hyperbole or a broad brush to depict a day of reckoning. We are responsible, he is saying, for the loving service we give or withhold from others in their need. On that and that alone will we be judged.

But the evidence will not, as some suppose, appear in a 'Book of Life' in which a recording angel has entered the specific acts of good and evil in our lives. Like the burden on Christian's back in *The Pilgrim's Progress*, our sins fall off at the cross and roll away, and we can forget them. We may, of course, be slow to repent but when we do, whether now or beyond the grave, we will not be kept waiting until the Last Judgement to be acquitted. Grace is waiting for us even before we ask for it. Nor is it a case of 'If you repent you will be forgiven'. Our repentance is not the condition of grace: it is, rather, our response to grace.

Then why should there be a Last Judgement at all, except for the final generation? Haven't we already come to judgement? And aren't we already in heaven, not only when we die but when we enter eternal life here and now? Once we have responded to the Word of God or knelt at the cross we have received Christ's peace and known that love from which neither things present nor things to come shall be able to separate us *(Romans 8:38-39)*. When St Paul at the end of 1 Corinthians 15 cries, 'Where, O Death, is your sting?', isn't he foreseeing an existence free from the agony of sin and guilt?

There is no room here for any belief in purgatory, a place of penance and purifying after death, as that has been traditionally understood. 'The official doctrine of purgatory', writes Simon Tugwell, 'is emphatically not a way of giving people a second chance, nor does it envisage any sort of posthumous finishing school or mental hospital, nor is it concerned to provide a nursery where dead infants can grow to maturity. It is strictly for people with unfinished penance.'[4]

Though a God of love does not consign his children to such a place of penance, a 'sort of posthumous finishing school' is less incredible. Charles Wesley's hymn, 'Love Divine' may say 'Finish then thy new creation:/Pure and spotless let us be'[5], and this is a legitimate aspiration; but it is not attained in this life. Here we advance slowly by way of much sinning and repenting; there, we will sin no more and advance, perhaps, by sitting like Mary at Jesus' feet *(Luke 10:39)* and by serving him in ways as yet unknown.

The idea of purgatory is not the only way in which the period between dying and the Last Judgement has been imagined. Some people believe that we will sleep until the trumpet sounds to announce the end of the world and history; others that we will inhabit a kind of celestial waiting-room.

The sleep theory has a basis in Scripture and in Jesus' time was accepted by the Pharisees but not the Sadducees. When Lazarus died, his sister Martha told Jesus 'I know he will rise again in the Resurrection on the last day' *(John 11:24)*. The disciples before Easter and St Paul before his conversion would have shared this belief. St Paul, in fact, did not abandon it until after his early letters to the Thessalonians *(see 1 Thessalonians 4:5-17)*. He was probably influenced by the expectation of Christ's imminent return. However, he came to believe that to die is to be with Christ *(Philippians 1:23)*. In any case it is obvious that you cannot believe, on the one hand, that the dead are in a limbo and, on the other, that we are surrounded by a great cloud of witnesses and that the communion of saints is a reality.

The waiting-room theory is equally implausible. This is St Augustine's doctrine of 'receptacles'; the belief that judgement will be deferred until the end of history and until then all souls are kept in appropriate receptacles. Surprisingly, this doctrine resurfaces in a twentieth-century theologian of repute, Oscar Cullmann, who argues in the closing pages of his *Christ and Time* that the dead are not yet raised. He, too, is throwing out belief in the communion of saints.[6]

In the Middle Ages the debate about heaven was vigorous and touched on essential and still controversial issues. In 1331, for example,

Pope John XXII argued from Matthew 25:34 that 'If it is only at the judgement that the blessed ones are told to take possession of the kingdom, it follows that they had not previously taken possession of it'. He also pointed out that if people are in fact rewarded or punished before their sentence is pronounced, everything is back to front!

Pope John succeeded in stirring up a famous controversy. Is there, or is there not, an in-between state which is not that of blessedness or beatitude? And is there one judgement, or two? Earth and heaven; or earth, an interim, and then heaven? From this controversy 'What survived into the later Western tradition', says Tugwell, 'was the doctrine of purgatory. Otherwise the essentially binary eschatology of the main tradition reasserted itself... There are essentially two stages, not three.'[7]

Tugwell also cites St Thomas Aquinas (1225-74), who favoured a two-stage eschatology. 'There is this life and the hereafter, not this life, the hereafter and then, as it were, the thereafter.'[8] St Thomas, however, believed that everyone's will is fixed immutably at death: so why should there be any delay in giving the souls of the dead their just deserts? Moreover, once beatitude is reached, there is nothing more to be desired, and there is no need for any further judgement. The views of Aquinas, however, are spoilt by the cut and dried theory of the unchangeable will, which we have already rejected by pointing to the injustice of pronouncing sentence on those cut off prematurely.

The theologians not only hold different views about these matters; they are in a complete muddle, and all of us are out of our depth. Is there an immediate judgement? If the rewards and punishments described by Scripture are handed out in our after-death state, that must be the case. Then what is there left for the Last Judgement? If, on the other hand, all is deferred, then those who, with St Paul, see death as falling into God's everlasting arms nurture false hopes. 'Saint Paul, wanting to be dissolved', says Tugwell, 'and Saint Ignatius, hastening to his martyrdom, quite properly expect results at once.'[9]

'He shall come again to judge both the living and the dead.' All the dead? Are the saints of the Old Testament, for instance, still, as they say, 'under the altar' awaiting this Day of the Lord? Or are they already redeemed? 'Glory', says Tugwell, 'is not the crowning of a successful life, nor is it the completion of a steady process of development. It is rather the imparting of success as a gift to people who had been struggling and often failing to lead an adequately human life.'[10] This could be the clue — a doctrine of redemption that does not just see ourselves continuing to grow but God fulfilling us with his glory and continuing in us his redemptive and creative work, so that, as Jesus promised to his disciples, our joy might be full.

Our puzzlement as to whether the judgement is at the beginning or the end may be due to our inadequate human perception of time and sequence. In eternity the Last Judgement may already have taken place. 'At what point', says Tugwell,

> 'do you hear a whole symphony? To hear it all at once within time would, of course, mean the most appalling cacophony. But even in time it is possible to hear a whole symphony, not just to hear a sequence of bits of symphony. The bits add up to a whole. Eternity is a sort of *tota simul possessio* [complete and simultaneous possession] enhanced far beyond our present comprehension.'[11]

Thank you, Simon Tugwell: you have helped at least one of your readers to understand. I can only appeal to other theologians who, with the Church as a whole, have failed to confront these issues, to give the further enlightenment which many intelligent but baffled Christians (and others) are seeking. The traditional teaching is confused and full of unresolved difficulties. But of one thing we can be certain. For the world and for ourselves the last word will be not judgement but grace. 'In the "Our Father"', as Hans Küng reminds us, 'we do not pray "thy judgement come" but "thy kingdom come"'.[12] God's kingdom, not his judgement, is the goal, the consummation that St John foresaw when he wrote in the Book of Revelation *(11:15)*:

> The kingdom of the world has become the kingdom of our Lord and of his Messiah, and he will reign for ever and ever.

1. J. A. T. Robinson, *In the End, God* (London: James Clarke, 1950) p. 71
2. Simon Tugwell, *Human Immortality and the Redemption of Death* (London: Darton, Longman & Todd, 1989)
3. Friedrich Schiller, 'Resignation', 1786
4. Simon Tugwell, *op.cit.*, p. 17
5. Charles Wesley, 'Love Divine' (Church Hymnary Book, Oxford Press)
6. Oscar Cullmann, *Christ and Time* (London: SCM Press, 1951)
7. Simon Tugwell, *op.cit,* p. 135
8. I*bid.*, p. 149
9. I*bid.*, p. 125
10. I*bid.*, p. 160
11. I*bid.*, p. 154
12. Hans Küng, *Eternal Life* (London: SCM Press, 1991)

8

The communion of saints

'Encourage us by their fellowship.'
Common Order of the Church of Scotland, 1994

The first word of the well-known spiritual 'When the saints go marching in' denies the conclusion we reached in chapter 7: it is not a matter of 'when'; the saints, all those who by God's grace have been accepted into heaven, are already in, apart from those still on earth. Yet the old misconception dies hard; which is why Stanley Spencer pokes fun at it in his famous painting, 'The Resurrection: Cookham'. He depicts the villagers, still unchanged at the final millennium, housewives in floral frocks and a bank manager in bowler hat and striped trousers, springing simultaneously from their graves. If this was an old discredited heresy he would not have bothered, but it was still alive in the twentieth century, so he did.

But if our dead are gloriously alive and awake with God they are not far from us. Whenever we lift our hearts to heaven, whenever at the Holy Communion or through the Word read, preached or sung we draw near to Christ, we are near to those who are with him beyond our sight.

It is not surprising that this is largely forgotten among Scottish Presbyterians. We are, save for the Celts, a somewhat phlegmatic and unmystical race. Visit the average Presbyterian congregation (not only in Scotland but worldwide) and you will rarely experience a sense of that glorious company of the dead who worship with us. In contrast, the Catholic monk reading vespers in his cell and the devout Anglican priest saying morning prayer in his church, sometimes with no other visible worshippers, have a strong sense of the unseen hosts.

It is extraordinary that the Church, with the major exception of the Eastern Orthodox Churches, does not make more of this. For many other Christians commemoration of the blessed dead, let alone communion with them, goes by default Sunday after Sunday. Yet church is the place above all others where those who have loved ones in heaven — a high proportion of every congregation — will be remembering them in moments of silence.

John Stone's hymn 'The Church's one foundation' is familiar to many people, though less often sung nowadays. The hymn describes communion with the dead, but when we sing it, do we believe it? We acknowledge the communion of saints in the Apostles' Creed, but it features inadequately in our worship and was omitted from the Church of Scotland's statement of faith in 1992. In its *Common Order* (1994), however, commemoration of the blessed dead, the plea that we may follow their example and the hope that when we die we may share with them the joys of heaven, is a constant feature. In the Communion services remembering them becomes fellowship with them, but perhaps this should happen more often, and the assurance that our loved ones are still bound with us in the love of Christ should be an essential part of every funeral service and a normal feature of Sunday worship.

I confess negligence. It was not until my first wife died that this aspect of belief became real to me. Seeking anonymity in a Scottish Episcopal church I found myself saying the Creed and the words 'the communion of saints' leapt out as never before. 'That is where she is', I told myself, 'and the saints are around us, and we are worshipping with them'. On the radio at that time I also heard a sermon by Professor James S. Stewart, then Moderator of the General Assembly of the Church of Scotland. It was a post-Christmas sermon on the text 'The angels were gone away from them into heaven' *(Luke 2:15)*. His final word was to the bereaved, and here, using a preacher's freedom, he calls those who have gone on ahead 'angels':

> 'Sometimes the angels are human angels. The angel left you ... all too soon, and it was as if the sunshine were suddenly obliterated. But ... God has recalled him, God has recalled her, into love and joy perpetual. And better still, remember this: the angels, though now unseen, are still singing somewhere yonder ... Listen when your heart is quiet... Angels, help us to adore Him!'[1]

That is how the communion of saints should be proclaimed. Why then, do so many churches evade the subject? There are, I believe, three explanations. The first is a matter of language. It is difficult for Reformed churches which do not use a liturgy to commemorate the dead, or constantly express their presence without becoming repetitive. But this can be avoided with the help of biblical and liturgical language, and set forms should not be despised.

Secondly, in its desire to repudiate the allegation that some Christians are so heavenly-minded that they are of no earthly use, the Church has become over-practical. That saying should now be put into cold storage. The greater danger now is not obsession with the life to come but becoming so involved in the state of the world that heaven, like God, is neither here nor there. The corrective is well stated by the fifteenth-century writer Thomas à Kempis, who gets the balance right: 'The sons of God standing upon the things that are present, do contemplate those things which are eternal. They look on transitory things with the left eye, and with the right do behold the things of heaven.'[2]

Thirdly, Protestants are afraid that if the communion of saints is stressed, it will lead to practices such as asking the saints for help and praying on behalf of the dead, which were rejected by the Reformers. But none of these difficulties are insuperable.

The belief that we are still in touch with the dead can become the spiritualist's assertion that we can communicate with them. But to be in communion is something different, and far more comforting than the enigmatic and frustrating messages delivered at a séance.

Does communion with the departed imply that we should pray for them? When the Church of England prepared its *Alternative Service Book 1980* there was disagreement over the petition 'Let light perpetual shine upon them and grant them your peace'. Many evangelical Anglicans protested that the dead were already in eternal light and peace, and that this prayer suggested that they were not. In spite of the reservation that if the dead are aware of earth's sorrows they know lack of peace, they do enjoy that peace which Jesus promised to those whose hearts are troubled (and which we too can enjoy amid the heartbreak of the world).

Though the dead are at peace, we can still pray 'Grant them your peace': it is an expression of our continuing love for them and the only kind of prayer we can utter. Even before they die we can often think of no particular blessing that our loved ones need, but that should not deter us from praying for them and holding them up in the love and peace of God. So too with the dead.

Those who pray this simple prayer are not thinking in terms of logic but opening their hearts; and this is far removed from the medieval notions of seeking merit for the dead and praying for souls in purgatory. It belongs to a higher conception of prayer, which goes beyond petition. For prayer, as P. T. Forsyth reminds us, is 'our supreme link with the unseen'. 'In Christ', he adds, 'we cannot be cut off from our dead nor they from us wherever they be. And this contact is in prayer.'[3]

Furthermore, says Forsyth,

> 'The instinct and custom of praying for our dearest dead ... should be encouraged and satisfied as a new bond for practical life between the seen and the unseen, where we have bonds all too few ... There is nothing serious that we may not bring to the Father ... And it is serious enough that half our heart, and all its treasure, should be snatched into the unseen.'[4]

In the hand of God, the dead no longer need our prayers. They do not depend on us, for that would disadvantage those who, for one reason or another, have no one to pray for them. When Dr Samuel Johnson in 1759 prayed for his mother it was not because her soul required his pleas, but simply because he loved her: 'I commend, O Lord, so far as it may be lawful, into thy hands, the soul of my departed mother, beseeching thee to grant her what is most beneficial to her in her present state.'[5]

Devotion to the saints and their use as intermediaries can be abused. But if we do not pray *through* them, we can pray *with* them. For the Church on earth and the Church in heaven are at one in adoring and serving God. Both are a part of the holy catholic Church. If the saints in light are not inactive but alive, then it is not mere speculation to say that they remember those whom they knew on earth in their prayers, and that the pilgrimage of the Church on earth is their concern. Nor are they now confined to another heavenly Church which absorbs all their interest. For there are not two bodies, the Church visible and the Church invisible: only one holy catholic Church. In its invisible aspect it includes the communion of saints; it might also be said that the Church invisible is inclusive of the Church here on earth.

There is therefore intercommunion between 'the saints' here and the saints yonder and we ought to remember them as they remember us, in prayer. And if we still ask what we are to pray for, we do not have far to seek. How natural, for example, was this prayer of Alan Paton's after the death of his wife:

> 'Grant that her life may unfold itself in thy sight, and find a sweet employment in the spacious fields of eternity ... Tell her, O gracious Lord, if it may be, how much I love her and miss her and long to see her again; and if there be ways in which she may come, vouchsafe her to me as a guide and guard and grant me a sense of her nearness as thy laws permit.'[6]

'Tell them that we love them still' are words that I have used both in worship and at the graveside. 'Comfortable words' like these should often be said.

When I plead with those who conduct worship to remember the communion of saints I sometimes feel that I am a lone voice; but I am comforted to know that it is not so. When the congregation of Greyfriars Kirk in Edinburgh published the sermons on worship preached by their minister, David Beckett, when that beautiful church was refurbished, I found in them this passage which sums up much of what I have been saying:

> 'Those in heaven are still very much aware of what is going on here, and very much involved in it. We affirm every week our belief in the Communion of Saints ... but within our own denomination I don't think that we have made enough of that great cloud of witnesses who still surround us and who still support us. The reaction against prayer for the dead was so strong at the Reformation, because of the abuses and the crude sale of indulgences that took place earlier, that for some years even funerals were barred; and Scottish people have been left without the quite legitimate support that faith in the life beyond death ought to give. It seems to me a very cruel thing to tell a newly widowed woman that she must not remember her husband in her prayers any more when probably she has been praying for him every day for fifty years during their marriage. It's not a case of trying to upgrade the departed ... but of being true to what we say the Church believes in ... The communion with the church in

> heaven opened up by worship is a factor that we have largely to take on trust at this stage; but this does not mean that it's not real.'[7]

The prospect of heaven is diminished when our dead are only a fading memory. It is enhanced when the communion of saints is a reality to us now, and when we know that on dying we will be received 'into the glorious company of the saints in light'.

1.   James S. Stewart, Radio Scotland (29 December 1963)
2.   Thomas à Kempis, *The Imitation of Christ*, Book III.38
3.   P. T. Forsyth, *This Life and the Next* (1918), p. 43
4.   *Ibid.*, pp. 43-6
5.   Samuel Johnson (1709-84), *Prayers and Meditations*
6.   Alan Paton, *Kontakion for You Departed* (London: Jonathan Cape, 1968) pp. 67-70
7.   David Beckett, *Worship* (sermons preached at Greyfriars Tolbooth Kirk, 1989)

9

Memory

*'You must remember the past if
you're to know where you're going.'*

Anon

'Let mental safari continue.'

William McIlvanney[1]

As we grow old, fragments of our childhood may resurface. Even so, the landscape of our past becomes increasingly indistinct. A mist or, for some, an impenetrable fog closes in.

Yet the dead remember. How do I know? Because memory is part of the self. And in heaven we cannot remain ourselves unless we either retain our memories or have them restored. To lose your memory entirely is to lose your identity. It is to be no longer responsible before God, unable to be judged or blessed, unable to enjoy him and to glorify him for ever.

In the developed countries today, where there is a greatly extended lifespan, we are more acutely aware of the gradual disabilities of age. Old people succumb less swiftly to fatal illness but slowly crumble in body and mind. 'Wrinklies' become 'crumblies', in the current jargon. While we may smile at this, we know that the degeneration of our memory cells, and especially the severe amnesia which culminates in senile dementia or Alzheimer's disease are no laughing matter. And when someone we love can no longer recognize us and sinks into a blank existence, our only solace is in saying, 'He is not himself any more'. Because he is not himself he is oblivious to much of what he would have suffered had he been less incapacitated, but he will never be himself again in this life, where tangles of protein formed in the brain make dementia irreversible.

If there is to be an afterlife for such a person in which he can enter into communion with his Lord or have any relationship with his loved ones, he must know something about his past and who he is. Otherwise reunion is impossible. None of us, for that matter, will be able to meet again with those whom we have not seen for thirty or fifty years unless we can recall our life together and appreciate all that makes our relationship special.

In this life memory is dependent on little grey cells; in the next life those cells will have gone, but what they contained will be preserved. Many of us will die with the old coat of our body tattered and torn; or, as Shakespeare put it, in

> 'second childishness, and mere oblivion,
> Sans teeth, sans eyes, sans taste, sans everything.'[2]

That coat or body will be gone, but we shall put on a new one, the same yet not the same, with attributes such as memory intact.

Yet this does not mean total recall. The sins of which we have repented and sought divine forgiveness are already forgotten, because we are absolved and shriven. How often we are told in the Bible that this is so; the symbolic scapegoat, the assurances of prophet and psalmist, and, above all, the words and the atoning death of Jesus, make it clear.

The afterlife can be heaven only if all that is discreditable is forgotten, the slate or tape of guilt wiped clean. Convicted murderers may make their peace with God, repent and receive absolution in the name of Christ. But in this life they are not allowed to forget: the families of their victims and the media will see to that. One can only hope and believe that in the life to come, when the families are delivered from their long agony and all malice and vindictiveness have ceased, the evil will indeed be forgotten.

And what of those tyrants, great and small, whose foul deeds follow them into eternity? Their hell may be to see the enormity of what they have done and have to live with it, unable to lay these ghosts but haunted by them until that day when, please God, they too may come to true contrition and forgiveness.

The subject of memory must be taken further. Astonishingly, it is a factor little mentioned, let alone discussed, in the literature concerning heaven or the theology of the last things. Yet it is of prime importance. If, as I maintain, memory is vital to our continuance as persons, and impaired and perished memories are to be restored, this would seem to suggest two propositions.

Firstly, that for all of us the capacity to remember will be greatly enhanced and our fragmented memories fully restored. This can only mean that our past lives from cradle to grave will be laid wide open; that the vast databank of memory will yield its secrets, hitherto withheld for lack of the full keyboard. We will recall vividly people and events, thoughts and feelings of long ago; but also discreditable episodes and states of mind which we have suppressed from a sense of guilt, embarrassment or shame. These will have to be faced and dealt with beyond death, if they have not already been atoned for and forgiven in this life. Those for which we have asked forgiveness will have been erased; the rest raise the question of judgement, with which I have already dealt.

And he who can restore our impaired memories will also deal with those other handicaps from which so many suffer, so that the blind will see, the deaf hear, the lame walk and the mentally afflicted become sane.

To recall with a new clarity will be to recreate and recapture the past. In this sense, if in no other, the saying 'You can't take it with you' is untrue. The elderly often wish they could remember the friends of their youth, the books they have read, the places seen, the moments of illumination when they were lifted out of themselves by something sublime. They may not recall that place or scene now, but with their memories rekindled they will.

Anita Brookner in her novel *A Closed Eye* describes the pain of a mother whose grown daughter has been killed. 'The main business of my life now', she says, 'is trying to recapture Imogen. Even your [her invalid husband's] face is a distraction, because when I am attending to you I am trying to see her face, which is puzzlingly out of reach.'[3] That is a common experience. The faces we most want to remember are almost always out of focus. In heaven, when we see them fully, we shall also have a clearer memory of their time with us on earth. Those we leave behind when we die may only recall us dimly but we shall recall them vividly.

The second proposition is that if memory persists it will be more than visual; we shall take with us aural memories and, indeed, those of all five senses: sight, hearing, smell, taste and touch. For memory embraces them all. I can still hear cowbells once heard on a Swiss hillside; still smell the scent of orange groves in Israel; still taste the nasty medicines of childhood; still feel the weight and texture of a cricket ball though I have not held one for many years. Traditional views of heaven exclude such things, because they belong to the physical world and so should be discarded. But memory retains them and such memories will, I believe, be more rather than less acute in heaven. Indeed, I have proposed total recall.

The thought that death does not entail sensual deprivation is precious. When the gypsy in George Borrow's novel *Lavengro* said 'There's a wind on the heath, brother ... who would wish to die?',[4] he assumed that death meant farewell to the touch of the breeze, and also to the song of the thrush, the scent of the rose, the taste of wine, the sight of the setting sun. But these sensual joys will not only live on in our memories but surely be surpassed. We shall be given an endowment as rich as or richer than the senses, objects as wonderful and more so, and subjects for our minds to feed on — for we shall not be mindless.

To speak of libraries in heaven sounds absurd, but there are living libraries already, deep in the human memory. One person can give you almost all the poems of Burns, another the full text of *Hamlet* or *Macbeth*. Don Quixote will ride again and Anthony Trollope's Barsetshire and the delicate world of Jane Austen will be recreated. Nor will those who have at their fingertips a century's record of sporting events and memories of their highlights have forgotten them there. I find it impossible not to see the afterlife in these terms, however wary one is of projecting earthly images.

If not only visual memory but these others persist, this could indicate the continuance of the senses themselves and point to a redefinition of the resurrection of the body. Like many other people, I have always interpreted the phrase 'the resurrection of the body' as meaning the resurrection of the identity or personality. But those from St Paul onwards who have used these words may be telling us that the dead are not ghosts, but sensitive beings and endowed with senses.

They are also sexual beings. We cannot shirk the subject of sexuality, for this is, like memory, an integral part of our make-up, our personal and not merely our animal lives. In human beings sexuality is more than physical. It is an endemic factor and whether it exists or not in the risen body it will continue to exist in the resurrected memory.

You will not find much about sexuality in books on the afterlife. Textbooks on Christian ethics however, now agree that it is given us neither, as was once held, for the sole purpose of procreation nor as an evil to be suppressed, but as a divine gift to be treasured and used responsibly. But not necessarily physically, for the sexual drive is sublimated in a variety of vocations and finds expression in many creative activities, especially in the arts.

We cannot tell what we shall be in heaven; what we shall not be is everlasting eunuchs or sexless beings. Purged of lust and aggression, meanness and pride, we shall retain the warmth and tenderness, the radiance and enchantment that are sexually inspired.

Memory is bound up with identity, with who we are. I am a Scot, born and bred in Scotland; and I shall take with me into heaven my love of Scottish voices and song, literature and culture, tradition and ethos. St John on Patmos saw the nations bring their treasures into the Holy City *(Revelation 21:26)* and all nations can still bring their treasures. Yes, we are all of one blood, but though this world becomes a global village and nations yield their sovereignty, we shall still, it is to be hoped, retain our own cultures and contribute our own treasure; but with no spirit of superiority or inferiority, no racism or exclusiveness.

Our sense of humour will also survive. The musical *Godspell* without blasphemy depicted Jesus as a clown, and made his humour known to a wide public. That this was an integral part of his personality is a guarantee, if any were needed, of laughter in heaven — a thought which our forebears would have regarded as frivolous. To go to meet our Maker, they would remind us — and we need to be reminded — is a solemn thing. But if they concluded that heaven had to be sombre, they were wrong. There will be much there to make us humble and penitent, but also much to make us merry. If W. S. Gilbert (of Gilbert and Sullivan) was right, and 'Life is a joke that's just begun'[5], then heaven will, among many other things, be a place of laughter.

Akin to humour is comedy, and in heaven comedians will continue to be comic. There are people so amusing that their very presence evokes laughter. Every primary teacher can point to some child and say, 'He (or she) is a wee comic', and it is a characteristic they may carry through life. Not all comedians belong to this category: offstage some are morose or disagreeable, or even tragically depressive and addictive. But those who are always amusing, the true drolls, will not become sedate and solemn in heaven.

Whatever human attributes persist (and there are many I have not mentioned), our God is like the householder to whom Jesus referred, who 'will bring out of his treasure what is new and what is old'

(Matthew 13:52). As well as retaining treasures which we have already been given, our lives will, I believe, be further enriched and endowed. This was beautifully expressed by Benjamin Franklin in the epitaph he composed for his tomb but which was never inscribed on it:

> 'The body of Benjamin Franklin, Printer, (like the cover of an old book, its contents worn out and stript of its lettering and gilding) lies here, food for worms. But the work itself shall not be lost for it will, as he believed, appear once more in a new and more beautiful edition corrected and amended by the Author.'[6]

The remembrance of all we have been given here through body, mind and spirit will fill us with praise. But at the same time we will remember this world's sorrows. Many who are in heaven will think of those they have left behind who are not coping well or are in great distress: children, perhaps, bereft of a parent; adolescents deprived of guidance; an aged parent who had been dependent on their support; or a weak partner whom they had strengthened or carried. How can they now enjoy untrammelled bliss in heaven? They may, of course, see the end from the beginning and know that all will be well. But on earth all does not always turn out well. Those children, full of promise, may fall into the hands of unloving guardians and be warped for life. Those teenagers, deprived at a crucial time of parental control, may get into deep trouble and never get out of it. That man or woman on the verge of alcoholism or drug abuse may, bereaved and lonely, become an almost hopeless addict.

If the dead have to look on, helpless, we can only say, with the author of Hebrews, 'They would not, apart from us, be made perfect' *(11:40)*; they cannot rest in eternal bliss until all earth's turmoil is done and its tragedies have ceased. Christ still weeps over Jerusalem, and those now with him will share his heartbreak for the sins and sorrows of the world.

There is, of course, another side to it. When my first wife died, some thirty years ago, our eldest daughter had scarcely begun her career and her sisters were still at school. I have often thought that some day I shall tell their mother how well their lives have turned out; their careers, their marriages, their children. But my guess is that she already knows. She could not remember us all without concern for our future, and she will either have foreseen that future or witnessed it as it occurred.

If the dead know about us we can be sure they pray for us. (That we should pray for them I have already affirmed.) And the thought of their prayers and their concern, pictured in Hebrews 12 as a great crowd of spectators at the arena, is one of marvellous encouragement. If we are concerned, as we should be, that we can still bring them sorrow, we should also remember our Lord's promise: 'You will know that I am in the Father, and you in me, and I in you' *(John 14:20)*. That communion is ours whatever we have to suffer; and those in heaven know it even more fully, and have a joy that neither sad memories nor continuing knowledge of this world can erase.

1.   William McIlvanney, *The Kiln* (London: Hodder & Stoughton, 1996) p. 207
2.   Shakespeare, *As You Like It*, Act 2 Scene 7
3.   Anita Brookner, *A Closed Eye* (London: Jonathan Cape, 1991) p. 243
4.   George Borrow, *Lavengro* (1803)
5.   W. S. Gilbert, 'Three Little Maids', *The Mikado* (1885)
6.   Benjamin Franklin, Epitaph for himself (1728)

10

Relationships

'What life have you if you have not life together?
There is no life that is not in community,
And no community not lived in praise of God.'

T . S. Eliot[1]

The nature of heaven is love, and if God is love and heaven is love we can say with certainty, though we have never been there, that it can be described as a realm of loving relationships. Christ's life of love confirms this. Because he was no solitary guru living in a cave in the hills where an élite few would seek him out, but kept company with men, women and children of all types and social classes, we know that a mark of heaven will be personal relationships. And because his concern was not confined to the salvation of the individual but to the founding of a church, a community, a kingdom, we know that heaven entails togetherness.

Is there anything more to be said? At this point the remarks of Dietrich Bonhoeffer ('On the borders it seems to me better to hold our peace'[2]) and John Baillie ('This is a region in which agnosticism is assuredly the better part of wisdom'[3]) suggest that we should come to a halt. Yet both advocate the doctrine of personal immortality and it seems right that anything we can say to establish this, and to remove obstacles, should be said.

Although heaven remains shrouded in mystery we can surely say, in the opening words of the First Epistle of John, 'We declare to you what was from the beginning, what we have heard, what we have seen with our eyes, what we have looked at and touched with our hands'.

For there is both God incarnate and also sufficient evidence in the past and present life of the world and in divine revelation to validate a heaven that is no mere shadowland.

Many people simply cannot believe that their puny lives — less than a speck in the eye of the universe — will survive. But over against this excessive humility we must set the mystery of human relationships. You may regard yourself as 'hardly worth a tinker's cuss', but you have relationships with others and it is in these that you truly exist. The relation between persons is what persons are. In Donne's phrase — and it takes a poet to seize the unforgettable metaphor — 'No man is an island entire of itself'[4]. Thus Margaret Thatcher, who notoriously declared that there is no such thing as society but only individuals, was wrong.

When we die, isolated from our past and unaware of what is to come, we seem to be alone; but this is an illusion. We take with us what we are, what all life's relationships and our responses to them have made us; and unless there is nothing ahead and we perish, there must be a community in which to live. We may exist in solitude but only in community can we truly live and love.

Prisoners or hostages consigned to solitary confinement only survive if, in lieu of any living relationship, their minds maintain contact with other minds, with words written or spoken in the past and the remembrance of other people. Those who sleep rough in a city do not survive only by scrounging cardboard coverings and scraping for food; unable to go it alone, they team up with one another. There are loners but these, deprived of relationships, may become disoriented or crazy. And if heaven were a kind of solitary confinement, in which we existed in isolation, we too would become less than human.

Heaven, then, is a community and it cannot be otherwise. A city, it is called, or the Holy City, the City of God. 'City' stands for community but not necessarily that of a metropolis. For many, cities are neither where they feel at home nor where they want to live. They may have spent their days on a secluded island or in a highland glen and would neither thrive in nor relish a large community. So be it. We need not worry about the multitude, for heaven has infinite space (if we can use such a concept as space) and its 'many mansions' are not to be equated with populous areas of living.

A life in community, in relationships: that is what matters. But community with whom? With those we have known and loved on earth, that's for sure. But we can hope and guess that there will be new friends as well, and especially for those who have known loneliness here, or who have been snatched by death before their time, so that all whom they love have been left behind.

If we already have many friends in heaven, we believe that those relationships, with which God has so richly blessed us, will continue. We have, by middle-age, acquired a vast network of relationships: not only family and friends but also members of the same congregation or social group; colleagues at work and at play; neighbours, and so forth. We glibly presume it is the same for everyone and that we will all settle with ease into the multiform relationships of heaven.

But it is not the same for everyone. Consider, for instance, those young people, not long out of school, who are pitched into the chaos of war and lose their lives. They have missed out on marriage and parenthood. They may not even have known an enduring friendship or a serious love affair. They enter the afterlife having lost out on so much of their earthly inheritance. When we meet them again will they still be so bereft? Will they still not know what such relationships mean? Or will the God who has given us so much and intended to give the same to them have restored to them 'the years that the locusts have eaten'(*Joel 2:25, Authorized Version*), so that they are not dispossessed nor has their unrealized potential, unfulfilled talents, uncompleted education, unsung music, gone to waste? Again we can only guess, and my own conjecture is that in the community of heaven, in ways we cannot foretell, they will have been given what was taken from them here. From our earthly perspective the promise of their lives went to waste; but in heaven that waste may be redeemed and all their promise fulfilled.

We expect, when we die, to mingle with our ancestors as well as the great and good from every generation. And why not? For if we are alive there, so will they be also. But our finite, earthbound minds again struggle with bafflement, the problem of how we are to know or even recognize one another.

In the first place, we can expect the spiritual body to resemble the discarded body; a continuity which the phrase 'the resurrection of the body' strives to express. In 1 Corinthians 15:53-54 and 2 Corinthians 5:4 St Paul clearly states that it is our mortal bodies that are to be raised. 'Our desire', he says (in Tugwell's paraphrase), 'is not to slough off mortality, but to have our mortality subsumed into eternal life.'[5]

Moreover, we are not, as the ancients thought, composed of body and soul as separate entities so that the one might be discarded and the other remain. The soul not only inhabits the body but expresses itself through it by voice and look and gesture. 'Body language' means not that the body speaks but that persons speak, even unintentionally, through their bodies. Spirit and body are intertwined, as I believe, forever.

And so, in the resurrection appearances of Jesus, his spiritual body bore a resemblance to his human body. It was not always a marked resemblance and in the garden *(John 20:14)* and on the Emmaus road *(Luke 24:16)* some of his followers had difficulty in recognizing him; but in one instance he showed his wounds *(John 20:20)*, and in another John recognized him on the shore *(John 21:7)*. Recognition beyond death is also contemplated in the gospels by Jesus' promise to the dying thief *(Luke 23:43)*, and to the disciples that they would again sit at table with him *(Matthew 26:29)*.

Inevitably there are unanswerable questions concerning, for instance, discrepancies of age. How can we resume our past relationships as if they had never been broken, when we ourselves, if not our dead, have changed with the passage of time? As Laurence Binyon said in the poem 'For The Fallen', 'They shall not grow old/as we that are left grow old'. In our memories the war-dead remain young, and this may be all that we mean; but, if they are indeed ageless, have we not grown away from them? Or take those grandparents whom we knew only when they were old and frail and we were children: will our heavenly relationship not be one of equality rather than dependence?

The afterlife cannot be a Tir-nan-Òg, a Celtic heaven of everlasting youth. Perpetual Peter Pans would be appalling. It is indeed a land of youth but in the sense implied by Jesus when he said 'Unless you become as little children...'. That is, unless you are humble enough to receive; unless you are not blasé nor cynical but responsive to love, goodness and joy; unless you keep the sense of wonder as fresh miracles surround you — you are already dead.

Medieval theologians thought that the dead would remain at the age of maturity, which they then reckoned to be in the thirties. (With slower maturation and greater longevity we might put it in the fifties.) I would rather accept Zechariah's vision, that in the Holy City there are children playing in the streets *(Zechariah 8:5)*. A heaven of lookalikes, with neither the freshness of childhood and youth nor the beauty of many an aged face does not ring true.

Anyone who has lost a child would like to know whether he or she will greet them as the mature person they should have become. Will there be some kind of playback of the lost years or, beyond time, will past and present coalesce?

'Beyond time' is a curious concept. It does not necessarily mean the annihilation of time. Eternity, though transcending time, may include it. 'Though God is not in time', says John Baillie,

> 'yet time is in Him and has meaning for Him. To take any other view would be to make the not unfamiliar mistake of regarding time as altogether illusory — to make the distinctions of before and after and of past and present *mean nothing*.'[6]

Baillie reflects that 'to contemplate the enjoyment by ourselves of an entirely non-successional life would be to claim for ourselves the prerogative of deity'. And he agrees with those who hold that, 'So long as the finite spirit remains finite, it must in some degree continue to experience reality under the forms of duration and succession'.[7]

Baron Friedrich von Hügel had the same conviction, that 'we ourselves shall never, either here or hereafter, be more than quasi-eternal, durational'.[8] If there is to be spiritual growth in heaven there must indeed be a distinction between before and after. Life there cannot be 'non-successional', but I am not certain that it needs to be durational and finite.

To arrive in heaven is to come home. But our pilgrimage will not have ended, and those who have gone before us will be further along the road. They will have changed 'from glory to glory'. This will in no way damage our relationship with them. On the contrary, they will love us with a greater and more understanding love. And problems of age-discrepancy will be resolved.

We are social beings existing in relationships with others. Therefore, I have maintained, we will continue to exist in a community. But I have also said that heaven is more than a community; to arrive there is to come home. For to be homeless in heaven is inconceivable. The God who on earth 'hath set the solitary in families' (*Psalm 68: 6, Authorized Version*) will do no less in heaven.

To be homeless in heaven would be like the sad fate of those millions on earth who mill around in vast refugee camps, displaced from their homes by war, famine or natural disaster. Their constant dream is to have a home of their own again.

When Jesus said to his disciples 'In my Father's house are many mansions' *(John 14:2, Authorized Version)* he was speaking directly to their condition. We no longer translate the Greek word *monai* as 'mansions'. After all, none of Jesus' neighbours in Nazareth, not even the rabbis, lived in a mansion; the nearest equivalent then would have been a Roman villa. Some inept interpreters have seized upon another possible translation, 'stages on the way', which, they tell us, combined with 'I go to prepare a place for you' suggests that Jesus saw himself as a kind of heavenly billeting officer going ahead to arrange the next camping-site for troops on the move. But heaven's 'stages' are those of our inner pilgrimage. We are not destined to pass from one transit-camp to another.

What Jesus said, as the modern translations make plain, is that there will be many dwelling places or rooms. There will be room for all, and all will find a home.

Sceptics, of course, will question the authenticity of these words from the Fourth Gospel. They will point out that, tape-recorders and even shorthand being far in the future, the discourses in the Upper Room *(John 14-17)* could only be a later compilation by the early Church. But could the Church invent such amazing words? The sceptics overestimate its capacity, but underestimate the retentiveness of the oriental memory, so much more acute than our own.

The most definite and authoritative statement ever made about heaven is in this passage, and beyond this we cannot go.

There are still questions to be asked but we are not given the answers. Questions, for example, about sharing that home in heaven with others. There is the family to which I belong by ties of blood; also my wife's family which became mine through twenty-six years of happy marriage. After her death I remarried and another family has become mine through another thirty years of happy marriage. Then there is the family of my children and grandchildren. Nor can I forget that my parents themselves had family relationships other than those of my childhood home. And the ramifications continue through all the relationships of my siblings and their families. Your situation may well be similar.

We are left wondering whether there will be any privacy in heaven, or how we shall cope!

We can only believe that with God all things are possible, and that in eternity there will be no question of which, of either/or, of this and not that. Where time is infinite you do not have to filch it from one person to give it to another. Within the infinite ramifications of every family there will be no exclusions or barriers but, beyond the restrictions of time, ever-widening circles of love and understanding; and permeating, binding together and transcending all these circles, the ever-present Christ.

1. T. S. Eliot, 'The Rock', *Complete Poems and Plays* (Faber & Faber, London)
2. Dietrich Bonhoeffer, *Letters and Papers from Prison* (London: HarperCollins, Fontana, 1959) p. 93
3. John Baillie, *And the Life Everlasting* (Oxford University Press, 1934), p. 198
4. John Donne, 'Meditation XVII'
5. Simon Tugwell, *Human Immortality and the Redemption of Death* (London: Darton, Longman and Todd, 1989) p. 105
6. John Baillie, *op.cit.*, p. 214
7. *Ibid.*, p. 225
8. Friedrich von Hügel, *Eternal Life*, quoted in Baillie's *And The Life Everlasting*, p. 227

11

Interpreting the signs

'Faith is interpretation.'

John Kelman[1]

Did the very young Robert Louis Stevenson really say, as he watched the lamplighter from his nursery window, 'Look, look, there's a man out there punching holes in the darkness'[2]? It sounds incredibly precocious even for Stevenson in his childhood.

This vivid metaphor describes the aim of my book. Look, I have said, at those who through flashes of illumination and faith, or promptings from above, have punched holes in the darkness that conceals the afterlife. And is not Jesus Christ, as he himself said, the light of the world? That light which, as St John puts it, 'shines in the darkness and the darkness has never mastered it' *(John 1:5)*. The darkness is that of this world; and Christ has brought us the clearest glimpse of a realm of light beyond all the clouds of our unknowing.

It is because I believe that Jesus is the light of the world and 'the image of the invisible God' *(Colossians 1:15)* that I see heaven as the inescapable consequence of the Christian faith. Belief in Christ also implies that the personal and loving God, the Father whom he revealed, will take care of our future as he keeps watch over us now. I am reminded of the words of a friend, written to me in his terminal illness:

> 'What awaits us now? I am very grateful to my father for once saying to me at a difficult time in my life, "The God who has taken so much care of you in the past, and has been so good to you, is certainly not going to throw you away now".'

'Our knowledge of God now' wrote Austin Farrer,

> 'is the promise and foretaste of heaven: apart from this present knowledge of God, we shall have no clue to what heaven will be; for heaven is God. But it's just as true the other way about — without the heavenly promises God has given us, we should have no understanding of our present life with God. How could we make sense of the journey if we didn't know where the road leads? Unless the promise of heaven was shown to us, how should we guess that the fitful gleams of spiritual light which visit us have flowed out from the steady and irresistible dawning of eternal day?' [3]

When that day dawns fully for us and we awake in heaven, what shall we see? According to Donne,

> 'there shall be no cloud nor sun, no darkness nor dazzling, but one equal light, no noise nor silence, but one equal music, no fears nor hopes, but one equal possession, no foes nor friends, but one equal communion and identity, no ends nor beginnings, but one equal eternity.' [4]

These much-loved words convey the tranquillity of heaven. Yet they do not bear close scrutiny. 'One equal light' would not satisfy the painter Rembrandt, the master of light and shade; 'one equal music', if this means the absence of conflict or even of harmony, would not please a musician. No hopes, no new beginnings and a cloning of identities? No; for if variety here on earth is the Creator's hallmark, Donne's picture is out of focus. The giver of colour and of the richness of our perceptions has provided signs of heaven both in nature and in all human endowment.

'Consider the lilies', said Jesus (*Matthew 6:28*), the wild flowers of the fields. The court of Solomon, the height of magnificence, lavish with silks and gold, precious stones and splendid garments and the work of craftsmen and builders of genius, was not dressed like one of them. 'If flowers had minds', reflects the Welsh poet R. S. Thomas,

> 'would they not think they were the colour
> eternity is, a window that gives
> on a still view the hurrying
> people must come to and stare at and pass by.' [5]

Those who stand and stare before they go, he is saying, glimpse heaven. I believe this.

Alfred Noyes, the poet, saw God in the face of his father coming from Holy Communion. Many who are familiar with funerals have observed the same thing. Not just the brave stoicism, nor the hysteria which sometimes sadly accompanies death; but grief transformed by faith, a radiance, and the indwelling Spirit of God — a clear clue, a manifestation and foretaste of heaven's glory.

How fascinating are the questions that remain, even if they are insoluble. When, for instance, I affirmed the survival of memory I asked about the other faculties with which we are endowed. One of these is inventiveness, which is innate in some natures but which all do not have to the same degree; another is the thirst for knowledge. In a scenario where all knowledge is revealed, there would be no scope for either discovery or research. But perhaps the scenario is different.

In his celebration of love in 1 Corinthians 13, St Paul says that prophecy *and* knowledge will vanish away. He probably meant religious knowledge, and that makes sense — there can be no room for the gropings of theology in the full light of the afterlife. But if he meant *all* knowledge, that is hard to accept. To be omniscient and know everything is to be the same as God. To know all is to cease from mental strife and that cannot be good. The true intelligentsia, those for instance on the highest levels of physics and mathematics, the researchers and academics, would have nothing to feed on, and would consequently become less interesting, lively and gifted there than here. And perhaps the simple-minded and the highly intelligent will become mentally equal. But if my friend who is not very bright were suddenly to become highly intelligent he would not be the friend I know and love. A heaven in which every angel is a clone of every other angel is not attractive. For these reasons I believe that intelligence will persist, and there will be fresh worlds of knowledge to conquer.

But if memory, inventiveness and the questing intellect persist, we are bound to ask whether every human quality and every characteristic that makes us individuals will likewise be retained. And if so, does this make heaven no more than a replica of earth?

But you have only to ask what we shall do in heaven to see that this cannot be so. Most of our earthly activities are by their very nature transient. In heaven we shall neither have to defend the peace nor establish law and order. Nor shall we pursue wealth or waste eternity in getting and spending. Even our most kindly concerns, such as charitable, social and medical work, will be inapplicable. We cannot even guess at our activities; but they will be radically different.

All we can say is that there will be tasks according to our needs. Unemployment and dead-end jobs here on earth are soul-destroying and therefore evil. But if death is the entrance to fullness of life there will be fulfilment for all — in Jesus' words 'life abundant'. Since heaven is a community and not a rabble, this will be found in community. A rabble is shapeless and disorderly; but a community has unity and shape and some form of government. Whether that will be entirely divine rule or whether we shall be given some part in it we cannot say. We only know that if any are given authority they will not exercise power but, as Jesus said, be like servants.

Into that heavenly community (of which the Church is meant to be the sign) will flow a never-ceasing stream of flawed humanity — the wounded and the deprived, the maladjusted and the abused, those with little education and many who on earth have been 'at the bottom of the heap'. There might be a field of service here, a role for carers, befrienders and educators.

But the question, 'What shall we do?' cannot be answered. We only know that 'his servants will serve him' and this may or may not involve serving one another. And we shall worship him — this, at any rate, is sure. A distinguishing mark of humanity is our capacity for worship. Here on earth, however, we do not find worship easy and have to practise the presence of God. In heaven we shall not have to practise that presence, for the clouds of our unknowing will be scattered. Living in his presence, it will not be difficult to pray. With all the company of heaven we shall glorify him and bless him for his unceasing goodness and love.

Even so, the prospect of perpetual prayer is a daunting one. But I do not believe we shall do nothing but pray. Whatever heaven is, it is not a monastery; nor is God like some arrogant ruler who requires the constant homage of his subjects. We shall fall on our knees, but he will tell us to stand on our feet and we shall see, if we do not already know, that worship is more than pious sentiments: it is self-giving — 'my utmost for his highest'; in heaven it is still hallowing his name in the way we hallow it on earth, by our words, attitudes, thoughts and deeds.

I will only add briefly, for I have said it already, that in heaven we shall intercede, for we shall not have forgotten those we have left behind.

Prayer is a part of the afterlife, not its whole. And since we can say so little about the rest, it is not surprising that so many of our contemporaries find it difficult to believe, or have at the most only a thread of hope. But we sometimes do less than justice to these sceptics. It is remarkable that, although they cannot make sense of the journey, they nevertheless show a resilience and enjoyment in living, a cultural depth and breadth of interests which are often lacking in their believing neighbour. They may also be dedicated to social and political ideals and the pursuit of justice without believing in, or caring about, any heavenly reward. Lord Boothby, for example, an acknowledged atheist as well as a libertine, confessed as his statement of belief that 'Courage and loving kindness are the infallible recipes for life ... compassion — the urge to diminish the sum of human suffering and to help those who are in difficulty, trouble or distress — brings the most abiding human happiness'.[6]

Many people would have discounted the chances of heaven for Joe Slovo, also an atheist (and a communist). But after his Jewish parents had died in the Holocaust he fled to South Africa, where he identified with the oppressed and worked fearlessly to destroy apartheid. He became the supporter and friend of Nelson Mandela, who appointed him Minister of Housing; and the rabbi who conducted his funeral compared him to the prophet Amos because he too defended the poor and spoke out against the inadequacies of the rich.

'Shalom, dear brother, Shalom, rest in peace', said the rabbi[7]. God, being who he is, will have said no less.

What is the point of trying to persuade such people? If they have a deep satisfaction in trying to make this world a better place and are content with their lot, should we not leave them to it? No — because they cannot speak with St Francis of 'kind and gentle death'. The death of their loved ones, even more than their own, brings only bleakness and unrequited pain. Old age, wrote Dylan Thomas, should not 'go gentle into that good night', but should 'burn and rave at close of day;/Rage, rage, against the dying of the light'.[8] Whether the life-affirming atheists are old or young, Thomas speaks to their condition.

What a contrast to the close of John Newton's life. When he was Rector of St Mary Woolnoth, in the City of London, he told a friend shortly before he died, 'I am packed and sealed and waiting for the post'; and to another who enquired about him he replied, 'I am like a person going a journey in a stagecoach, who expects its arrival every hour and is frequently looking out at the window for it.'[9] Even before old age is upon us, that readiness and composure have been, from the early martyrs onwards, the truly Christian response to death — although not all of us who are Christians have attained it.

The lives of millions in this world are 'solitary, poor, nasty, brutish and short'[10]. What comfort or recompense is there for them if the atheists are right and there is neither God nor heaven? This life would be rotten at the core. And so it is, unless we see the mystery of our existence through the eye of faith; unless like Jacob we awake and say, 'Surely the Lord is in this place — and I did not know it!' *(Genesis 28:16)*.

To many people the words *mystic* and *mysticism* suggest something remote and inaccessible but what they mean is interpreting the otherness in the ordinary. Faith, Kelman said, is interpretation. This insight delivered me from a period of agonizing over whether I should offer myself for the ordained ministry. I had held back, waiting for some mystical call and doubting whether I had sufficient faith. My real failure, I found, was not interpreting the signs through which God had been prompting me for a long time.

We have not only to interpret but to receive. For the God in whom we believe is not distant and aloof. A remote, passive and indifferent deity would not be worth believing in. He would be inferior to the best of his creatures.

The Christian God, however, is one who gives himself, has spoken and speaks. This is not anthropomorphism, the heresy of creating him in our own image and heaven according to our own preferences — the presumptuous thought that he is like us. It is the perception that his goodness and generous love are the same attributes that we know but written large, larger than we can conceive. We ask, with one of the great hymnists of the twentieth century, Canon G. W. Briggs:

> 'Shall God not share his children's care
> If such a heart as mine their sorrow heedeth?
> Can my poor love Rise high above
> The love of Him from whom all love
> proceedeth?'[11]

Unbelievers lack awareness of the living God either because the Church in the poverty of its discipleship has failed them, or because they have made themselves deaf to its true voice. (Jesus still says, 'He who has ears to hear, let him hear.') Those who are cut off from the Church and what they regard merely as institutionalized religion are at a great disadvantage here. For God makes himself known in this fellowship of believers, in the acts of shared worship, in sacraments infused with holy mystery, in preaching which proclaims Christ, and in those deeds of compassion where he is present ('you did it to me').

It is then that we know the truth of what C. H. Dodd called 'realized eschatology'. The 'last things' are now; the kingdom for which we pray and the heaven beyond death have already come in Jesus Christ. What awaits us there is already here. We can know eternal life now. 'Eschaton Now' on hoardings, rather than the much-ridiculed 'The End is Nigh', would really be saying something. For, yes, the kingdom of God is at hand.

1. John Kelman (1864-1929), Minister of Free St George's, Edinburgh, 1907-29
2. Denis Duncan, The *Daily Telegraph* (23 March 1996)
3. Austin Farrer, *A Celebration of Faith* (London: Hodder & Stoughton, 1970) p. 122
4. John Donne, *XXVI Sermons* (1660)
5. R. S. Thomas, 'Flowers', in *Collected Poems* (Bordon: Phoenix, 1993) p. 390
6. Robert Rhodes James, *Boothby. A Portrait* (London: Headline, 1991)
7. The Rabbi at Joe Slovo's funeral, January 1995
8. Dylan Thomas, 'Do not go gentle into that good night', in *Collected Poems* (London: J. M. Dent)
9. Bernard Martin, *John Newton* (London: Heinemann, 1950) p. 357
10. Thomas Hobbes, 'Leviathan' (1651)
11. G. W. Briggs, 'Shall God Not Share', *Enlarged Songs of Praise* (Oxford University Press, 1931) Hymn 638

12

Into glory

'They are all gone into the world of light.'

Henry Vaughan[1]

I consider that the sufferings of this present time are
not worth comparing with the glory about to be revealed to us.

Romans 8:18

When my friends die I cross out their names in my address book. A friend of mine did not do that: she only changed their addresses to 'Gone to glory'. In the Salvation Army, in a similar way of speaking, it is often said that someone has been 'promoted to glory'.

What is glory? It is on every page of our hymn books, but is it just a vague word with neither definition nor content?; like the teenager who, asked what he thought of some entertainment, replies 'Brilliant!', which tells you little except that he was impressed.

Are 'glory' and 'glorious' words like that, merely talismans of enthusiastic faith? Or are they something more, even in their common use? A glorious day, for instance, is more than a sunny day. The latter may be windy and cold or oppressively humid; but a glorious day is one in which everything comes together — temperature and light, colour and clarity, sun and cloud, earth and sky. So when we speak of heaven as the realm of glory it is not a vague description. Heaven is the perfect unity, the bringing together of all that is good and beautiful, holy and true.

When St John wrote of Jesus that he 'lived among us, and we have seen his glory' *(John 1:14)* he was, perhaps, recalling that night on the mountain when Jesus' face 'shone like the sun, and his clothes became white as the light' *(Matthew 17:2)*. His glory there was of a heavenly nature, the glimpse of another, more perfect existence. And that, according to St Paul, is for us all. We all reflect Christ's glory and are being transformed into his likeness with ever-increasing glory *(2 Corinthians 3:18)*. What does this mean but that all that is good in us (and given by God) will predominate, while the sins and sinfulness that hinder us will be purged away. This surely is what heaven and purgatory are all about.

'And the glory of the Lord shall be revealed'. Handel's setting of these words in the *Messiah* is more illuminating than any wrestling with the word glory. In the same way the many references in the Bible to the glory of God — in his transcendence and his presence — are to be experienced rather than analysed.

With the whole Church we pray, 'Thy will be done on earth as in heaven'. We are to reflect, anticipate and echo heaven as we do God's will; and in our obedience we shall glimpse the glory. But, as those opposed to the Church never tire of telling us, we have an inglorious record; or, as we freely concede, an extremely chequered one.

However blemished, the Church is constantly doing God's will. It is his agent of mercy in a suffering world. It fights the battles of the poor and deprived, befriends the lonely, comforts the distressed, opposes tyrannies, heals the wounds and overcomes the enemies of humankind; and silently, like yeast in bread dough, it influences souls without number. All this is a sign of the glory to come.

In word and worship too there are more than hints of glory. The words of Scripture have a power above other words to open the heart and mind to God; and sermons inspired by these words can enlighten us and change our lives. Said or sung by a congregation, the Apostles' and Nicene Creeds and the Te Deum are charged with glory, as are many prayers, although it must be confessed that we are better at praying for others than at adoration. I have already written of how the sacrament of Holy Communion anticipates heaven: it is also a present experience of glory.

It is when we trivialize worship, when the Church tries to be 'with it', when God is 'chatted up' in the prayers, when reverence and dignity are sacrificed to affability and 'fellowshipping', when some charismatic experience is sought rather than God himself — above all, when we focus on our human needs rather than on the triune God — it is then that the glory escapes us. In trying to make God accessible we can forget he is the Almighty. The writers of the Book of Psalms never made that mistake. In the psalms God is both exalted and familiar; Jesus used them as his prayer book and was at home with them. And we should cherish the language of worship, avoiding what is artificial or precious as well as what is too colloquial; and whether the Bible is in ancient or modern words, they should be words that retain the wonder and power. The glory of eternal things, heaven's glory, must, as far as we are able, be gloriously expressed.

In heaven we shall see and experience that glory not only in the threefold being of God, Father, Son and Holy Spirit, but also reflected in all that is there. And because this is the only adequate description of heaven, we should handle it with humility and reverence.

Handle it with humility, because like unborn infants we cannot foresee what lies ahead. We can only, as the infant cannot, anticipate and try to interpret the signs. We cannot predict, we can only guess. And we should also be aware of the danger of thinking in terms which are too definite and concrete.

To visualize the immaterial is, of course, impossible. And you can understand the difficulty felt by many who are put off ideas of an afterlife because it is not a material reality.

The difficulty is increased when we realize that innumerable human joys are wedded to materiality: the joys of the senses, which I have already mentioned; physical activities, from walking and gardening to every kind of sport; mental pursuits such as reading and studying; handiwork, from engineering to the arts; homemaking — the list is endless. Since every pure joy bears the stamp of its divine Maker, and expresses his love, it is difficult to imagine any of these being thrown on the scrapheap, the mere debris of a world which one day will cease to be. Yet how can they find a place in eternity without their material form? Literature may survive in the memory but can there be any living literature without books? In heaven there will be even more wonderful blessings from the Creator, yet this huge question remains unanswerable.

We cannot tell whether there is some kind of material continuity between the pleasures of earth and those of heaven, as there apparently is between our physical bodies and those bodies that await us. Unsophisticated people who have retained the wonder and imagination of children, as Jesus told us to, often think so. 'One of my dreams of heaven', an old lady — a sparkling, unsolemn 'secular saint' — told me, 'is hot buttered scones! For I believe that all nice things come from God, and must be foretastes of heaven.' She may be right.

To Robert Browning it is the essence, rather than the outward appearance of earthly joys that will be preserved: 'All we have willed, or hoped or dreamed of good shall exist; not its resemblance but itself'.[2]

John Donne, similarly, says that 'when we shall see God, *sicuti est*, as he is, we shall see all things *sicuti sunt*, as they are; for that's their essence as they conduce to his glory'.[3]

But we should be content to leave such questions in the hands of the God of surprises. 'Don't you want to know about heaven?' a child was asked. 'No', she said, 'I want it to be a surprise.' And that, perhaps, is why so little is revealed. We are meant to say 'Heaven alone knows' and leave it at that. Before the mystery of death we must therefore be reticent. And however convincing we find the intelligibility of the universe, the beauty of creation and the hints and guesses, as well as the manifestations and revelations of eternity, we must not become obsessive in our enthusiasm. We must rest in our certainty rather than incessantly dwelling on it. We do not have to go on reminding ourselves that Jesus saves or that we are forgiven, so also we do not have to go on about heaven.

Nor does a fuller awareness of the validity of prayers for the dead mean that we should intercede for them night and day. How wise Luther was when, in preaching on prayers for the dead, he pointed out that you should believe that your prayer is answered after praying once or twice in case you mistrusted God. If we keep on praying for the same thing it is a sign that we do not believe.

Showing restraint means not clinging to our dead. They belong there, not here. ('Do not cling to me', said Jesus to Mary in the garden in John 20:17.) And there is comfort in the thought so beautifully expressed by the Quaker, William Penn, in the opening words of his prayer: 'We give back to you O God those whom you gave to us. You did not lose them when you gave them to us, and we do not lose them by their return to you.'[4]

I cannot foresee the mainstream churches becoming obsessed with heaven, yet for over-pious people the temptation can be real. Bonhoeffer knew this, and in his *Letters and Papers from Prison* he cautioned thus: 'For a man in his wife's arms to be hankering after the next world is, in mild terms, a piece of bad taste, and not God's will.' He added:

> 'God will see to it that the man who finds him in
> his earthly happiness and thanks him for it does not
> lack reminder that earthly things are transient, that

it is good for him to attune his heart to what is eternal, and that sooner or later there will be times when he can say in all sincerity, 'I wish I were home'. But everything has its time, and the main thing is that we keep step with God, and do not keep pressing on a few steps ahead — nor keep dawdling a step behind.'[5]

I have suggested that the Church, as a whole, is lagging behind. It is unlikely to outrun the gospel in its eagerness for heaven. Yet some of us may outrun the gospel's restraint in our eagerness to know what awaits us. Such eagerness is misplaced: our concern should rather be for God and his will, focussed not on our own destiny but, as all Christian faith should be, on the person of Christ, and his kingdom.

Here again, simple people often have a truer perspective than learned theologians. The man, woman or child for whom religion is 'taking Jesus by the hand' and who says from their heart 'What a friend we have in Jesus' is not likely to be excessively transcendental, whereas the great Karl Barth, as Evelyn Underhill remarked, was 'too exclusively transcendent and abstract, carrying the revolt from naturalism too far'. 'It's worth while', she added,

'to reflect on what happens when the whole emphasis of religion is thrown on the transcendental and eschatological. The majority of people must have something to lay hold of, and if it isn't given them by the incarnational and sacramental path, uniting supernature with homeliness, they just vulgarize supernature and claim familiarity with it.'[6]

Neither Barth's rarified spirituality nor an unseemly familiarity with holy things is acceptable. For most of us the latter is the more likely shortcoming. In everyday speech, in an irreverent age, the word God is everywhere abused. We say 'O God!', 'By God!', or simply 'God!' without thinking. If challenged we would reply that such expletives don't mean anything; they only add colour. But those of us who do not swear do not refrain because of some old-fashioned taboo but because it devalues the spiritual coinage, and God and heaven become less real. The third of the Ten Commandments, honoured by Jews more than by Christians, is wise: 'You must not make wrong use of the name of the Lord your God' *(Exodus 20:7, REB)*. God and heaven require reverence and to be irreverent is to forget that we are created beings.

The true attitude is the positive one called for by a 1993 statement of the World Conference on Faith and Order held in Santiago: 'We need', it said, 'an inclusive spirituality which recognizes that human beings are but a part of God's astonishing creation.' Reverence, that is to say, both towards God and, as has become increasingly recognized, towards our whole environment.

To value humility and restraint does not mean banishing spontaneity and joy; joyful dancing and singing are not necessarily irreverent.

All our thinking about heaven and earth must be laced with humility and reverence. Job, regarding the marvels of creation, says 'These are but the outskirts of his ways' *(Job 26:14)*. And Isaiah *(55:9)* reminds us that God's thoughts are not like ours:

> For as the heavens are higher than the earth,
> so are my ways higher than your ways
> and my thoughts than your thoughts.

We cannot solve the eternal mysteries, nor claim more knowledge than God has been pleased to impart. It is good that this is so. If we could know everything we would lose faith and mystery and the pilgrim spirit; we would cease to adventure, to launch out into the deep. If heaven were an open book we could go on to gain all knowledge and our pride would know no bounds. Far better is the course of the righteous, which according to Scripture is 'like the light of dawn, which shines brighter and brighter until full day' *(Proverbs 4:18)*, heaven becoming ever more real until 'the day breathes and the shadows flee' *(Song of Solomon 2:17)*.

Meanwhile I take my stand with Baillie, Bonhoeffer and many others who have reflected deeply, when they acknowledge that little can be said but that we can affirm in faith and hope that we have an eternal destiny. And this the Church should hold before our eyes, along with the reality of the saints whose presence and example will enable us to live more faithfully as feebler followers of Jesus. And it should say to us, as Jesus said to Thomas, 'Do not doubt but believe!' *(John 20:27)*.

John Baillie never stopped declaring from the pulpit, where it is often left unsaid, that we are on our way to heaven. And at the close of a book so full of quotations — deliberately so, for one man's thoughts on heaven are of little weight, whereas the consensus of many can less easily be denied — I want to quote him again, this time from a sermon:

> 'Somewhere, somewhen, somehow we who are
> worshipping God here will wake up to see Him as

He is, and face to face; but where or when we know not, or even whether it will be in a "where" or a "when", that is, in space or time at all. No doubt it will all be utterly different from anything we have ever imagined or thought about it. No doubt God Himself will be unimaginably different from all our present conceptions of Him. But He will be unimaginably different only because He will be unimaginably better. The only thing we do certainly know is that our brightest hopes will be more than fulfilled, and our deepest longings more than gratified. We can be certain that there will be nothing to disappoint, however much there will be to surprise.'[7]

'There is a land of pure delight'[8], wrote Isaac Watts in the same spirit of ardent anticipation. He prefaced his hymn with the words 'The Prospect of Heaven', and if that sense of eager expectation were restored to our worship it would raise the hearts of many who walk in shadows and encourage a serene and confident spirit in the hesitant.

Watts's full inscription is 'The Prospect of Heaven makes Death easy', which is not entirely true, for the cutting of earthly ties, if only for a while, is far from easy. But with the prospect of 'a house not made with hands, eternal in the heavens' (2 Corinthians 5:1) the sting of death was drawn for St Paul and his faith was strengthened. Paul cannot be written off as a head-in-the-clouds mystic. The mystical and practical, heavenly-mindedness and earthly competence struck a perfect balance in him. He knew as little of the afterlife as the rest of us; but he was able to assure his hard-pressed fellow-Christians at Corinth, 'For this slight momentary affliction is preparing us for an eternal weight of glory beyond all measure' (2 Corinthians 4:17).

I have written of that glory and I wish that others would do the same. My hope is that this small book may act as an incendiary device ticking away on the lower shelves of theology and in due time exploding, to kindle insights and illuminations beyond my own in the minds of hitherto neglectful theologians.

Little more can be said about heaven. There are plenty of hints and guesses, but these alone will not convince the Doubting Thomases, nor will any amount of argument. For their real doubt is not about heaven, but about God: and this can be resolved in other ways.

I understand their difficulty. To catch the infinite in our little net seems incredible. But the good news (which is what the word 'gospel' means) is in the New Testament, which focuses on the doubters' situation, especially in the accounts of the seeker Nicodemus and the doubter Thomas *(John 3, 20)*.

Nicodemus was a religious leader but had found little joy in orthodox religion. He was trapped in a system of religious beliefs and traditions and strict and demanding moral codes, and was drawn to Jesus because he wanted to be freed and find a living God. Jesus told him that he could make a new start (be 'born again'), and also that God's Spirit was as real and knowable, though as mysterious, as the wind. 'You hear the sound of it, but you do not know where it comes from or where it goes' *(John 3:8)*.

Meteorology has now removed some of the mystery, but it is still a potent image: God is as real as the wind. 'All right,' says the doubter 'I can feel the wind; but I don't feel God.' You can only feel the wind, I reply, when you go out in it. When your door is shut and you are cocooned with double-glazing, you can ignore it. But you only have to look out of the window to tell that it is there. Branches are bending, dead leaves falling and litter is blowing about on the street.

We know the wind by what it does, and we know there is a God by what he does. The analogy could be carried further, for like the wind he bends our stubborn wills, rids us of useless prejudices and burdensome traditions and sweeps the litter of pollution and ugliness from our lives. And if we open our eyes we shall see him doing this in the world.

The evidence of deeds is more compelling than any argument. In what to many is the greatest biblical book of all, the Fourth Gospel (John's Gospel), Jesus says just this. 'If I am not doing the works of my Father, then do not believe me. But if I do them, even though you do not believe me, believe the works' *(John 10:37-38)*. And again: 'Believe me that I am in the Father and the Father is in me; but if you do not believe me, believe the works' *(14:11)*.

If the doubter is to cease doubting he must also take the way of Thomas. It was his scepticism which gave birth to the phrase 'a Doubting Thomas'; which is a pity, for St John is less interested in Thomas's doubts than in the fact that he became a believer (and went on, it is said, to become the apostle to India).

How did it happen? The story (told in John 20:24-29) is of contemporary importance, for it suggests how our doubts can be dissolved.

One interpretation of Thomas's absence from the upper room when Jesus appeared to his disciples (an interpretation which echoes how many people feel towards the Church today) is that, understandably,

Thomas had cut himself off. There was a developing community of the Resurrection, but it was not for him. He would be embarrassed and feel he was there under false pretences; it would be more honest to remain apart.

But Thomas was mistaken, and so are they. A friend, perhaps, persuaded or brought him. He came, he saw and he was conquered. It was not only the wounds, but far more the presence of Jesus that convinced him. And in finding his Lord he found his God.

This is the way for us — to go with Thomas to the meeting-place. I have always been impressed by the way in which many people have come to believe through the Student Christian Movement and the Iona Community, for these are organizations which demand no prior commitment. Doubters and enquirers are welcomed; but there is a strong nucleus of those who believe, and Christ is there at the heart of things. The Church, too — any church — should be like this: Christ-centred, but open and welcoming to all, whatever their doubts or difficulties. 'Come for water, all who are thirsty' is the true note of Scripture (*John 7:37*); and Jesus laid down no conditions when he said 'Come'. As he welcomed Thomas he also said, 'Happy are those who find faith without seeing me' (*John 20:29*). When we have made the leap of faith and trusted in his promise that where even two or three meet together in his name he is there, we cease to ask for proof.

Belief in an afterlife has a firm foundation, for it springs from faith in God: in what he is and what he does. These are made evident supremely in the Resurrection, but also in the words and deeds, then and now, of Jesus Christ. I believe in a Christlike God. I believe in him through the life, death, resurrection and continuing ministry of Jesus Christ. And I believe that he is able 'to accomplish abundantly far more than all we can ask or imagine' (*Ephesians 3:20*). Therefore I believe in heaven.

And that the glory shall be revealed.

1. Henry Vaughan, *Silex Scintillans* (1620; 1655)
2. Robert Browning (1812-89), 'Abt Vogler'
3. John Donne, *Sermon at Lincoln's Inn* (1620)
4. William Penn, quoted in *The Oxford Book of Prayer* (OUP, 1985) p. 163
5. Dietrich Bonhoeffer, *Letters and Papers from Prison* (HarperCollins, Fontana, 1959) pp. 56-7
6. Evelyn Underhill, *Letters* (16.8.33, 25.8.33) (London: Darton, Longman & Todd)
7. John Baillie, 'When I awake', in *Christian Devotion* (Oxford University Press, 1962) pp. 82-3
8. Isaac Watts, 'There is a land of pure delight' (*Church Hymnary*, third edition) hymn 536

Acknowledgements

I am grateful to the Revd Jean Stewart of Islay for so willingly and skilfully typing the first manuscript, to Katharina Nimmo for the final typing on to disk, and to my wife for her constant encouragement and help.

Scripture quotations, unless otherwise stated, are from the *New Revised Standard Version* of the Bible, copyright 1989 by the Division of Christian Education of the National Council of the Churches of Christ in the USA, and are used by permission. All rights reserved

The extract from Dag Hammarskjöld's *Markings* (1964) is reproduced by permission of Faber and Faber Limited

The extract from David Lodge's *Paradise News* (Secker and Warburg, 1991) is reprinted by permission of Reed Books

The extract from John Burnaby's *The Belief of Christendom: A Commentary on the Nicene Creed* is reproduced by permission of the Society for the Promotion of Christian Knowledge

The extracts from T. S. Eliot's *Complete Poems and Plays* are reproduced by permission of Faber and Faber Limited

The extract from Philip Callow's *Van Gogh: A Life* is reproduced by permission of Allison & Busby Ltd

The extracts from *Collected Poems* of R. S. Thomas are reproduced by permission of J. M. Dent

The extracts from John Baillie's *And the Life Everlasting* are reproduced by permission of Oxford University Press

The extract from Iris Murdoch's *The Black Prince* is reprinted by kind permission of the author; © Iris Murdoch 1973

The extract from David Attenborough's *Life on Earth* is reproduced by permission of HarperCollins Publishers Ltd

The extracts from William McIlvanney's *The Kiln* is reproduced by permission of Hodder and Stoughton Limited

The extract from Axel Munthe's *The Story of San Michele* is reproduced by permission of John Murray (Publishers) Ltd

The extract from C. S. Lewis's *Letters to Malcolm* is reproduced by permission of HarperCollins Publishers Ltd

The extract from Edgar Jones' *The Triumph of Job* is reproduced by permission of SCM Press Ltd

The extract from J. S. Stewart's *A Man in Christ* is reproduced by permission of Hodder and Stoughton Ltd

Other Titles From WGP

SONGBOOKS with full music (titles marked * have companion cassettes)
LOVE AND ANGER*, John Bell and Graham Maule
WHEN GRIEF IS RAW, John Bell and Graham Maule
THE LAST JOURNEY - PACK OF 15 OCTAVOS* John Bell
THE LAST JOURNEY reflections*, John Bell
THE COURAGE TO SAY NO: 23 SONGS FOR EASTER & LENT*John Bell
and Graham Maule
GOD NEVER SLEEPS – PACK OF 12 OCTAVOS* John Bell
COME ALL YOU PEOPLE, Shorter Songs for Worship* John Bell
PSALMS OF PATIENCE, PROTEST AND PRAISE* John Bell
HEAVEN SHALL NOT WAIT (Wild Goose Songs Vol.1)* J Bell & Graham Maule
ENEMY OF APATHY (Wild Goose Songs Vol.2) J Bell & Graham Maule
LOVE FROM BELOW (Wild Goose Songs Vol.3)* John Bell & Graham Maule
INNKEEPERS & LIGHT SLEEPERS* (for Christmas) John Bell
MANY & GREAT (Songs of the World Church Vol.1)* John Bell (ed./arr.)
SENT BY THE LORD (Songs of the World Church Vol.2)* John Bell (ed./arr.)
FREEDOM IS COMING* Anders Nyberg (ed.)
PRAISING A MYSTERY, Brian Wren
BRING MANY NAMES, Brian Wren

CASSETTES & CDs (titles marked † have companion songbooks)
Tape, LOVE AND ANGER, † Wild Goose Worship Group
CD, THE LAST JOURNEY, † John Bell (guest conductor)
Tape, THE LAST JOURNEY, † John Bell (guest conductor)
Tape, IONA ABBEY, WORSHIP FROM EASTER WEEK (ed/arr Steve Butler)
Tape, THE COURAGE TO SAY NO † Wild Goose Worship Group
Tape, GOD NEVER SLEEPS † John Bell (guest conductor)
CD, GOD NEVER SLEEPS † John Bell (guest conductor)
Tape, COME ALL YOU PEOPLE † Wild Goose Worship Group
CD, PSALMS OF PATIENCE, PROTEST AND PRAISE † Wild Goose Worship
Group
Tape, PSALMS OF PATIENCE, PROTEST AND PRAISE † WGWG
Tape, HEAVEN SHALL NOT WAIT † Wild Goose Worship Group
Tape, LOVE FROM BELOW † Wild Goose Worship Group
Tape, INNKEEPERS & LIGHT SLEEPERS † (for Christmas) WGWG
Tape, SENT BY THE LORD † Wild Goose Worship Group
Tape, FREEDOM IS COMING † Fjedur
Tape, TOUCHING PLACE, A, Wild Goose Worship Group
Tape, CLOTH FOR THE CRADLE, Wild Goose Worship Group

DRAMA BOOKS
EH JESUS...YES PETER No. 1, John Bell and Graham Maule
EH JESUS...YES PETER No. 2, John Bell and Graham Maule
EH JESUS...YES PETER No. 3, John Bell and Graham Maule

PRAYER/WORSHIP BOOKS
THE PILGRIMS' MANUAL, Christopher Irvine
THE PATTERN OF OUR DAYS, Kathy Galloway (ed.)
PRAYERS AND IDEAS FOR HEALING SERVICES, Ian Cowie
HE WAS IN THE WORLD: Meditations for Public Worship, John Bell
EACH DAY AND EACH NIGHT: Prayers from Iona in the Celtic Tradition, Philip Newell
IONA COMMUNITY WORSHIP BOOK,
THE WHOLE EARTH SHALL CRY GLORY, George MacLeod

OTHER BOOKS
THE OWL AND THE STEREO, David Osborne
COLUMBA: Pilgrim and Penitent, Ian Bradley
THE EARTH UNDER THREAT: A Christian Perspective, Ghillean Prance
THE MYTH OF PROGRESS, Yvonne Burgess
WHAT IS THE IONA COMMUNITY?
PUSHING THE BOAT OUT: New Poetry, Kathy Galloway (ed.)
EXILE IN ISRAEL: A Personal Journey with the Palestinians, Runa Mackay
FALLEN TO MEDIOCRITY: CALLED TO EXCELLENCE, Erik Cramb
REINVENTING THEOLOGY AS THE PEOPLE'S WORK, Ian Fraser

WILD GOOSE ISSUES/REFLECTIONS
A VERY BRITISH MONSTER: A Challenge to UK Immigration Policy, Stanley Hope
A FAREWELL TO THE ARMS TRADE, Bernadette Meaden
CELEBRATING SAINTS: Augustine, Columba, Ninian, Ian Fraser
COMPASSION IN THE MARKETPLACE, Joy Mead
SURPLUS BAGGAGE: The Apostles' Creed, Ralph Smith
THE APOSTLES' CREED: A Month of Meditations, David Levison
WOMEN TOGETHER, Ena Wyatt & Rowsan Malik